THE *Homestyle* AMISH KITCHEN COOKBOOK

HARVEST HOUSE PUBLISHERS
EUGENE, OREGON

Unless otherwise indicated, Scripture quotations are taken from the New King James Version. Copyright © 1982 by Thomas Nelson, Inc. Used by permission. All rights reserved.

Verses marked KJV are taken from the King James Version of the Bible.

Cover by Dugan Design Group, Bloomington, Minnesota

Cover photo © iStockphoto / Camrocker

Every effort has been made to give proper credit for all stories, poems, and quotations. If for any reason proper credit has not been given, please notify the author or publisher and proper notation will be given on future printing.

THE HOMESTYLE AMISH KITCHEN COOKBOOK
Copyright © 2010 by Harvest House Publishers, Inc.
Published by Harvest House Publishers
Eugene, Oregon 97402
www.harvesthousepublishers.com

Library of Congress Cataloging-in-Publication Data
   Varozza, Georgia
   The homestyle Amish kitchen cookbook / Georgia Varozza, general editor.
      p. cm.
   ISBN 978-0-7369-2858-8 (pbk.)
   1. Amish cookery. 2. Amish—United States—Social life and customs. I. Title.
   TX715.V335 2010
   641.5'66—dc22
                                                                            2009029460

All rights reserved. No part of this publication may be reproduced, stored in a retrieval system, or transmitted in any form or by any means—electronic, mechanical, digital, photocopy, recording, or any other—except for brief quotations in printed reviews, without the prior permission of the publisher.

Printed in China

11 12 13 14 15 16 17 18 / RDS-SK / 10 9 8 7 6

CONTENTS

INTRODUCTION
5

BREAKFAST TREATS
7

BREADS, ROLLS, AND DOUGHNUTS
35

SOUPS AND STEWS
73

SALADS AND DRESSINGS
93

VEGETABLES AND SIDE DISHES
113

MAIN DISHES AND CASSEROLES
137

DESSERTS
189

MIXES AND MISCELLANEOUS
243

SUBSTITUTIONS AND MEASUREMENTS
265

RESOURCES
267

INDEX
269

Bless my kitchen, Lord, and light it with love. As I plan and cook my meals, keep me ever mindful of the wonderful benefits that come from serving my family. I pray, Lord, that my loved ones will feel Your presence and rest content in Your grace and provision. Amen.

*She brings her food from afar.
She also rises while it is yet night,
And provides food for her household…
A woman who fears the Lord, she shall be praised.
Give her the fruit of her hands,
And let her own works praise her in the gates.*

Proverbs 31:14-15,30-31

INTRODUCTION

I come from a long line of good cooks, Plain and otherwise, and many of the recipes in this cookbook have been handed down in my family for generations. Other recipes were gleaned from friends at the Conservative Amish Mennonite Church that I attended.

For as long as I can remember, the women in my family (and even some of the men) have enjoyed time spent in the kitchen preparing meals for those we love. Some of these recipes weren't written down, but instead passed down as the daughters worked alongside mothers, learning by doing. Certainly, that's how my sisters and I learned, and by the time we were teens, we were knowledgeable and efficient in the kitchen, and we loved turning out goodies on a weekly basis. Our cookie jar was never empty. Mama also felt strongly that her daughters would learn, among other things, how to turn out a perfect crust, and I still love to bake pies as a result of her careful instruction.

My mother raised four girls and one boy (who is an excellent cook also), and Christmastime was especially enjoyable for us. For weeks beforehand we'd gather daily in the kitchen and turn out all sorts of special baking that would find its way into gifts for neighbors and anyone who showed up unexpectedly at our door, with plenty left over for us. Oftentimes, on long winter evenings, my mother and father would crack sacks of walnuts harvested from my grandfather's trees, while my sisters and I sat at the kitchen table and copied and recopied family recipes or played board games. Dad would more than likely pop a big pan of popcorn and top it with melted butter and salt—what a treat that was! We'd talk and work and eat, and those memories of the family gathered around the kitchen table are precious to me even after many years.

Family lore has it that during the Depression our grandmother issued a standing invitation to the extended family. Every week after church, the whole clan would gather at her table for a big meal. Sometimes this was the only good meal some of the relatives could look forward to all week, and Grandmother always made sure there were plenty of leftovers to send home with the aunts and uncles and cousins. Because they lived on a farm, my grandparents were able to be generous in spite of the lean times. Mama said they were as poor as church mice right along with everyone else, but food was plentiful and they were openhanded.

When I raised my own family—I have three

grown boys—I was so thankful that my mother had taught me the joys of cooking up love in the form of good food, because sometimes it seemed as if I spent all my time in the kitchen. I always kept a large garden, and we had a small fruit orchard and 53 blueberry bushes that I tended. We raised chickens for eggs and meat, turkeys, hogs, sheep, rabbits, and angora and milk goats. I canned anywhere from 400 to 600 jars of food each season to help see us through the winter, and I froze and dehydrated many pounds of produce as well. We didn't have store-bought bread, and while raising my children, I ground wheat and rolled oats to use in my bread baking. I usually made four loaves at a time, and one loaf was always made into cinnamon sugar bread, which we would take from the oven and devour on the spot. I took such joy in being able to take care of my family with the fruits of my labor.

The recipes you will find in this book are the recipes my children were raised on. Good, solid food that "fills in the cracks," as we like to say. My sons are grown now, with wives and families of their own, and every one of them cooks. I love it when one of my boys calls me up to ask me a cooking question—they may not realize it, but they have begun making memories of their own.

In this fast-paced world, there are few things better than taking the time to prepare the ingredients for a great meal and gathering the family around the table to enjoy the results. For a short while, our cares and responsibilities fade into the background, and we can focus on our families, delighting in the small news of the day and savoring the pleasure that comes from a lovingly prepared home-cooked meal. I hope that some of the recipes in this book will find a place in your kitchen, and that as you prepare your family meals you, too, will take pleasure in the simple art of cooking for loved ones.

Blessings!
Georgia

BREAKFAST TREATS

Morning comes early for the Amish. Often rising as early as 4:30 a.m., the males in the family head to the barn to care for the many animals usually found on an Amish farm. There are cows to milk, horses and pigs to feed, and eggs to gather from a flock of chickens. So much to do! Morning chores can easily take an hour or more. It's easy to work up quite an appetite.

Meanwhile Mother and the girls fire up the cookstove and begin breakfast preparations. The morning meal is important for Amish families. It must feed them and keep them going for many hours of steady work—the noonday meal is a long way off.

The breakfast table is also the place where the adults discuss their plans and schedules for the day, where scholars fuel themselves for the hours of learning ahead, and where the first silent prayer of the day is shared by all.

Without a word, Father bows his head, and the family follows. Again without a word, Father begins to serve himself from the many plates and bowls on the table. Prayer time is over. Now it's time to dig in and eat up.

Breakfast is served!

Joy comes in the morning.
Psalm 30:5

Lord, I thank You that Your mercies are new every morning. What an encouragement that is! As I begin this new day, may I be mindful of Your love for me. Help me to pass that love on to everyone I interact with today—to my family, friends, and strangers. Open the eyes of my heart that I might see the needs of others. I pray, Lord, that You will use me today to lighten someone's load and to remind them that You are faithful—great is Your faithfulness!

Amish Breakfast Casserole

1 lb. bacon, cut up

1 onion, chopped

6 eggs, beaten

4 cups hash browns, thawed and shredded

2 cups Cheddar cheese, shredded

1½ cups cottage cheese

1¼ cups Swiss cheese, shredded

In a large skillet, brown the bacon and onion, stirring, until bacon is crisp; drain.

In a large mixing bowl, mix together the remaining ingredients and then stir in bacon mixture. Transfer to a greased rectangular baking dish and bake, uncovered, at 350° for 35-40 minutes or until eggs are set. Let stand 5 minutes before cutting.

Amish Breakfast Pizza

1 lb. sausage

1 batch biscuits, unbaked

1 cup potatoes (use shredded fresh or frozen)

1 cup Cheddar cheese, shredded

5 eggs

½ cup milk

½ tsp. salt

¼ tsp. pepper

Cook the sausage until browned; drain.

Grease a jelly roll pan and pat the biscuit dough in the bottom of pan. Spoon the sausage over the dough and then spread the potatoes and cheese on top.

Mix together the eggs, milk, salt, and pepper. Pour over the pizza and bake at 375° for 25-30 minutes or until done.

Notes:

Any housewife, no matter how large her family, can always get some time to be alone—by doing the dishes.

Notes:

Amish Coffee Cake

2 cups brown sugar

2 cups flour

¾ cup shortening

1 tsp. baking soda

1 cup hot coffee

1 egg

2 tsp. vanilla

Mix together the brown sugar, flour, and shortening just until mixed; there will be lumps. Take out 1 cup of sugar and flour mixture and set aside to be used later for a crumb topping.

Dissolve the baking soda in the hot coffee and add to the remaining flour mixture. Add the egg and vanilla and mix quickly; do not overmix.

Pour batter into a rectangular baking dish and sprinkle on crumb topping.

Bake at 350° for 30 minutes; turn to 325° if top starts to get too brown.

Remove from oven and sprinkle with powdered sugar or leave plain.

Apple Cinnamon Granola

4 cups rolled oats

½ cup coconut

1 cup nuts, finely chopped

½ cup sesame seeds

¾ tsp. salt

1 tsp. cinnamon

½ cup honey

⅓ cup oil

½ tsp. vanilla

1 cup dried apples, finely cut

Combine the oats, coconut, nuts, sesame seeds, salt, and

cinnamon in a large bowl. Combine the honey, oil, and vanilla separately and then add to the first ingredients.

Mix thoroughly. Spread out on 2 greased cookie sheets and bake at 350° for 20-25 minutes, stirring occasionally.

Cool, and then add 1 cup finely cut dried apples.

Store in tightly covered container.

Apple Fritters

1 cup sifted flour
1½ tsp. baking powder
¼ tsp. salt
1 T. sugar
½ cup milk
1 T. oil
1 well-beaten egg
2 apples, peeled, cored, and sliced

Sift together flour, baking powder, salt, and sugar. Blend together milk, oil, and egg. Gradually add to the dry ingredients. Stir in apples.

Fry in butter or oil, just like you would pancakes.

Serve plain or with powdered sugar.

Apple Oatmeal

1 cup rolled oats
2 cups cold water
½ tsp. salt
1 finely chopped apple
dash each of cinnamon and nutmeg

Combine the oats, water, and salt in a saucepan and cook 10 minutes on low heat. Then add the apple and spices and cook 5 minutes more or until apples are done to desired softness.

Serve with brown sugar, honey, or cinnamon sugar, and milk.

Notes:

Bacon, Egg, and Cheese Casserole

½ lb. bacon
6 slices bread
½ lb. Velveeta cheese
6 eggs
2 cups milk
½ tsp. salt
¼ tsp. pepper

Fry bacon until crisp and then crumble into pieces.

Cut bread into cubes and place in a well-buttered 2-quart casserole dish. Cube cheese and layer on top of bread cubes. In a mixing bowl, beat eggs, milk, salt, and pepper. Pour over the bread and cheese. Sprinkle bacon pieces on top. Cover and refrigerate overnight.

Bake covered at 350° for 50-60 minutes or until puffed up and golden.

Basic Granola

6 cups rolled oats
2 cups (any combination) raw walnuts and sunflower seeds
¾ cup honey
1 T. salt
¾ cup vegetable oil
½ cup water
3 tsp. vanilla
2 cups raisins
2 cups toasted wheat germ

Mix all ingredients together except for raisins and wheat germ. Spread in thin layer on cookie sheets or large baking pans. Bake for 1 hour at 300°.

When cool, add the raisins and wheat germ.

You can also add coconut, dried apricots, or dried apples.

Store in airtight container. The granola will last longer if stored in the refrigerator.

Berry Muffins

1¾ cups flour
1 cup + 1 T. sugar, divided
2½ tsp. baking powder
½ tsp. cinnamon
¼ tsp. salt
1 cup milk
¼ cup butter, melted
1 egg, beaten
1 tsp. vanilla
1 cup berries (blueberries, cranberries, blackberries, etc.)

Grease muffin pans. Preheat oven to 375°.

Stir together in a large bowl the flour, 1 cup sugar, baking powder, cinnamon, and salt.

In another bowl stir together milk, butter, egg, and vanilla. Add to the dry ingredients in the large bowl and stir just until blended. Batter will be lumpy. Fold in berries.

Fill muffin cups ¾ full. Sprinkle with remaining sugar. Bake for 20 minutes or until done.

Blackberry Syrup

1 cup blackberry juice
1½ cups sugar
1 T. lemon juice
¼ cup light Karo syrup

Put all ingredients in a saucepan and bring to rolling boil. Boil one minute. Remove from heat and skim off foam. Store leftover syrup in refrigerator.

Notes:

Plans for marriage are kept secret in Amish communities. But one can get an idea of who might be marrying come the autumn wedding season by looking at the family garden to see how much celery is planted—celery is an important element of Amish weddings and is used much the same as bouquets of flowers are used in English weddings.

Notes:

Blueberry Oatmeal Muffins

1 cup flour
2 tsp. baking powder
½ tsp. salt
½ tsp. cinnamon
½ cup brown sugar
¾ cup rolled oats
1 egg
1 cup milk
¼ cup melted butter
¾ cup blueberries, fresh or frozen
sugar for sprinkling

Stir the flour, baking powder, salt, and cinnamon together. Add the sugar and rolled oats and mix well.

In a large bowl, beat together the egg, milk, and butter. Add dry ingredients and stir until just moistened. Fold in blueberries.

Fill muffin tins about ⅔ full and sprinkle a bit of sugar on top of each muffin. Bake at 375° for 20 minutes or until brown.

Breakfast Crunch Bars

1 cup oatmeal
1 cup cornmeal
3 cups whole wheat flour
½ cup sugar
2 tsp. baking powder
1 tsp. soda
2 tsp. salt
1½ cups milk
¾ cup molasses

Kids especially love this treat. You can also crumble the crunch bars into a bowl, add milk, and eat like cereal.

Mix together the dry ingredients. Then heat the milk, add the molasses, and mix the milk mixture with the dry ingredients.

Pour into a lightly greased baking dish and bake at 350° for 25-30 minutes. Cool completely before slicing into bars or, while still hot from the oven, eat with milk as you would cereal.

Bubbat

1½ cups milk
2¼ tsp. (1 package) active yeast
3 T. sugar
1 egg, beaten
1 T. salt
3½-4 cups flour
1 lb. sausage

Scald milk and cool to lukewarm in a large mixing bowl; then add yeast and sugar. Let stand until bubbly. To the yeast mixture add the egg, which has been beaten, salt, and enough flour to make a soft dough that can barely be stirred with a wooden spoon.

Let the dough rise, covered with a towel, until it doubles in size.

Place the dough in a greased rectangular baking dish and press in the sausage at regular intervals. If you are using ground pork sausage, you can lightly brown it first to render out a bit of the fat. If using link or smoked sausage, cut into 2-inch lengths and press into the dough.

Let the dough rise again until it almost covers the sausage pieces.

Bake at 375° for 45 minutes or until done.

Buckwheat Pancakes

2 cups buckwheat flour
2 eggs, beaten
2 tsp. sugar
2 tsp. baking powder
⅛ tsp. salt
1½ cups milk
½ cup water

Mix together all ingredients. Drop the batter on a well greased, hot griddle and cook the pancakes until they are brown, then turn and cook second side until done.

Notes:

Buckwheat has a nutty, robust flavor. If you prefer, you can use 1 cup buckwheat flour and 1 cup regular flour in these pancakes for a slightly less distinct taste. I always grind my buckwheat groats as I need them, and I believe this helps the taste to be sweet.

Notes:

Buttermilk Biscuits with Sausage Gravy

Biscuits

2 cups flour

½ tsp. salt

3 tsp. baking powder

½ tsp. baking soda

3 T. shortening

1 cup buttermilk

Sift together dry ingredients. Cut in shortening until mixture resembles coarse crumbles. Add buttermilk all at once. Mix with a fork until it forms a ball. Turn out the dough onto floured counter and knead for 30 seconds. Roll out the dough until it's ½-inch thick and then cut with a biscuit cutter.

Place biscuits on an ungreased cookie sheet and bake at 425° for 15 minutes.

Sausage Gravy

1 lb. sausage

4 T. flour

1 quart milk

salt and pepper to taste

Brown the sausage in a heavy saucepan or iron skillet with sides. Do not pour off the grease. Add the flour and mix, stirring constantly. Add the milk and continue to stir while the mixture comes to a boil and thickens. Add a bit more milk if it's too thick. Salt and pepper to taste.

Tear or cut biscuits in half and ladle gravy over the top of the biscuits.

Buttermilk Pancakes

2 cups flour
6 T. powdered buttermilk
1½ tsp. baking soda
1 tsp. salt
2 eggs, beaten
2 cups water
¼ cup melted butter

Thoroughly mix together dry ingredients. Add remaining ingredients and stir lightly just until dry ingredients are moistened. Mixture will be thick and lumpy. Grease a skillet or griddle using a mix of butter and oil for best taste, and drop batter a tablespoon at a time onto the hot skillet, spreading the batter with a spoon. Cook the pancakes until they are golden and then turn and cook until the other side is browned.

Notes: *You can substitute 2 cups buttermilk and 1 tsp. baking powder for the powdered buttermilk and water.*

Cheesy Breakfast Casserole

1 package frozen Tater Tots or hash browns
8 oz. Velveeta cheese, cubed
6 eggs
¼ cup milk
salt and pepper to taste
½ cup ham, cubed

Grease or butter a 9 x 9-inch casserole dish and place a layer of Tater Tots over the bottom. Next, layer on the Velveeta cheese.

Whisk together the eggs and milk and season with salt and pepper. Pour over the Tater Tots and bake at 350° for 45 minutes. Remove from oven and sprinkle the ham over the top; return to oven for another 15 minutes or until eggs are completely set.

Notes:

Some Amish families still make use of ice houses to see them through the hot summer months. In winter, families will cut blocks of ice and store them, covered with sawdust, in well-insulated ice houses. They place the ice in the top compartment of their refrigerators; as the ice slowly melts, the cold water streams down the back into a catch basin and the air inside is kept cool.

Corn Fritters

2 cups fresh or frozen corn (thawed, if using frozen)
2 eggs, beaten
¼ cup flour
1 tsp. salt
⅛ tsp. pepper
1 tsp. baking powder
2 T. heavy or light cream
4 T. butter or oil (you may need more)

Mix together the corn, eggs, flour, salt, pepper, and baking powder. Add the cream and mix well again.

In a heavy frying pan or skillet, melt the butter and drop corn mixture by spoonfuls into the hot grease. Brown both sides, turning once. Serve plain or with maple syrup.

Cornmeal Mush

3 cups cold water
1 cup cornmeal
1 tsp. salt

Mix together all ingredients and bring to a boil, stirring constantly. Cover and simmer on low heat for 20 minutes. (If the heat is turned up too high the cornmeal will stick to the bottom of the pot and burn.)

You can serve it up into bowls at this point and eat it like a porridge or put it in a loaf pan and set in the refrigerator until chilled. Then cut it in slices and fry in bacon drippings or oil until golden on each side.

Cottage Cheese Fritters

2 cups cottage cheese
2 eggs
½ cup milk
2 cups flour
4 tsp. baking powder
1 tsp. salt

Mix together all ingredients and drop by rounded teaspoonful into oil to cover. (You can use a deep-fat fryer or a deep, heavy skillet.) Drain on paper towels and eat plain, with pancake syrup, or with powdered sugar.

Cottage Cheese Pancakes

1 cup cottage cheese
4 eggs
½ cup flour
¼ tsp. salt
¼ cup oil
½ cup milk
½ tsp. vanilla

Mix together all ingredients until well blended. Fry on a lightly greased griddle.

Cracked Wheat Cereal

3 cups cold water
1 tsp. salt
pat of butter
1 cup cracked wheat

Bring water, salt, and butter to a boil. Slowly add cracked wheat, stirring while adding. Cover and simmer on low heat for 20-30 minutes.

Notes:

You can make your own cracked wheat by coarsely grinding wheat berries.

Notes:

Creamed Eggs on Toast

4 T. butter

4 T. flour

2 cups milk

4 hard-boiled eggs, peeled and chopped

salt and pepper to taste

In a medium saucepan, melt butter on medium-low heat. Add flour and whisk while adding so the flour doesn't become lumpy. Continue whisking the flour/butter mixture while adding the milk. Continue to stir until mixture just comes to a boil and thickens. Remove from heat and add hard-boiled eggs and salt and pepper to taste. Spoon over toasted bread.

You can easily make a larger batch of creamed eggs if you're feeding a lot of people by simply doubling this recipe, but if eggs are limited, you can get away with only 6 eggs for a double batch.

Drop Biscuits

2 cups flour

4 tsp. baking powder

½ tsp. salt

5 T. shortening

1 cup milk

Sift together the flour, baking powder, and salt into a bowl. Cut the shortening into the flour mixture until it is completely incorporated. Make a well in the center and pour in the milk all at once. Stir with a fork until well mixed. The dough will be quite soft.

Drop by heaping tablespoons onto a greased baking sheet and bake in a preheated 450° oven for 15-20 minutes.

Dutch Babies

2 eggs
½ cup milk
½ cup flour
½ tsp. salt
pinch of nutmeg (optional)
2 T. butter
2 T. powdered sugar for dusting

Place a 10-inch cast-iron skillet or heavy frying pan with sides inside oven and preheat oven to 475°.

Meanwhile, in a medium bowl, beat eggs with a whisk until light and frothy. Add milk and stir. Gradually whisk in flour, salt, and nutmeg.

Remove skillet from oven and reduce oven temperature to 425°. Melt butter in hot skillet so that the bottom and sides are completely coated with butter. Pour the batter into the skillet and immediately return to oven.

Bake at 425° until puffed and lightly browned, about 12 minutes. Sprinkle with powdered sugar and serve immediately, either plain or with maple syrup.

Easy Buttermilk Pancakes

2 cups flour
1½ tsp. baking soda
1 tsp. salt
2 eggs, beaten
2 cups buttermilk
¼ cup butter, melted

Thoroughly mix dry ingredients. Add remaining ingredients. Stir lightly to just moisten dry ingredients. Mixture will be thick and lumpy. Drop by tablespoons onto lightly greased griddle, spreading batter with spoon. Turn cakes as soon as browned on bottom. Cook until other side is browned.

Notes:

You can easily double this recipe if you have a larger frying pan.

Old-fashioned buttermilk resulting from churning butter is quite unlike store-bought cultured buttermilk. It's thin and slightly watery, with "flakes" of butter floating in it, and has a sour taste. But old-fashioned buttermilk makes the best buttermilk pancakes you can imagine. Rich, buttery, and light. Yum!

BREAKFAST TREATS

Notes:

Most Amish homes raise chickens for meat and eggs. If you don't have access to "home-grown" eggs, buy free-range brown eggs at the store. You can taste and see the difference.

Fastnachts

2 cups milk
½ cup shortening
¾ cup sugar
1 tsp. salt
2 eggs
2¼ tsp. (1 package) active dry yeast
2 T. warm water
7 cups flour, more or less
powdered sugar

Bring the milk and shortening to the boiling point but do not boil. Turn off heat and stir in sugar and salt; cool to lukewarm. Beat eggs and add to the milk mixture.

Dissolve the yeast in 2 T. warm water. Let stand till slightly bubbly and then add to the milk mixture.

Sift and measure the flour and then add enough to the milk mixture to form a soft dough that can be handled easily. Knead the dough for 5 minutes. Put in the refrigerator overnight.

In the morning, roll out the dough to ¼-inch thickness and cut into 2-inch squares. Make a slit in the center of each square. Cover with a towel and let rise for ¾ hour.

Fry in deep fat until golden brown. While still warm, roll in powdered sugar.

Four-Week Refrigerator Bran Muffins

6 cups ready-to-eat bran cereal, divided

2 cups boiling water

1 cup shortening or butter

1½ cups sugar

4 eggs

1 quart buttermilk

5 cups flour

5 tsp. baking soda

1 tsp. salt

raisins or nuts (optional)

Place 2 cups bran cereal in a bowl and pour in the boiling water. Set aside to cool. Meanwhile, cream together the shortening or butter, sugar, and eggs. Add to the butter mixture the buttermilk and the now-cool cereal mixture.

Sift together the flour, baking soda, and salt and then add that to the creamed mixture and fold until the flour is moistened. Fold in an additional 4 cups *dry* bran cereal.

Store batter in covered container in refrigerator. Keeps 3-4 weeks. When ready to bake, preheat oven to 400° and fill well-greased muffin tins ⅔ full. Bake for 20 minutes or until done.

Raisins or nuts can be added to the muffin batter just before baking.

Notes:

Notes:

Grandma's Granola

2 cups whole wheat flour

6 cups rolled oats

1 cup coconut

1 cup wheat germ

1 T. salt

½ cup water

1 cup oil

1 cup honey

2 tsp. vanilla

Combine dry ingredients in a large mixing bowl. Blend liquid ingredients and then add to the large bowl and mix thoroughly. Spread out on 2 greased cookie sheets and bake at 250° for 1 hour, or until dry and golden.

Store in covered container.

Grape Syrup

4 cups grape juice

½ cup sugar

¼ cup cornstarch

In a large saucepan, combine 3½ cups of the grape juice and the sugar and heat until boiling.

In a small bowl, combine the cornstarch with the remaining ½ cup grape juice. Whisk into the grape juice and sugar and continue to whisk and cook until the mixture thickens. Cool to room temperature. Serve over pancakes or waffles.

Homemade Graham "Nuts" Cereal

3½ cups whole wheat flour
1 cup brown sugar
1 tsp. salt
1 tsp. baking soda
1 tsp. ground cinnamon
2 cups buttermilk
2 tsp. vanilla

In a large bowl, combine all ingredients and mix well. Pour out onto an oiled 12 x 16-inch flat, low-sided baking pan and spread evenly with a spatula. Bake at 350° for 20 minutes or until the batter is firm, medium-brown in color, and has begun to shrink away slightly from the sides of the pan. With a metal spatula, completely loosen the hot patty and allow to cool on a rack for several hours.

Preheat oven to 275°. Break patty into chunks and put through a meat grinder or a food processor until coarse crumbs are formed. Divide crumbs between two 12 x 16-inch pans.

Bake for 30 minutes, stirring every 10 minutes. Let cool and then store in airtight containers.

Serve as a cold cereal with milk.

An excellent breakfast treat. Eat this and you'll never want to buy store-bought cereal again.

Homemade Maple Syrup

1 lb. brown sugar
½ cup white sugar
1 cup water
⅔ cup light Karo syrup
2 tsp. maple flavoring

Combine all ingredients and heat until dissolved. Keep leftover syrup in refrigerator. If it crystallizes in the refrigerator, heat gently to dissolve the sugar when next used.

Notes:

Hush Puppies are a very old recipe, guaranteed to fill you up for pennies. On cold winter mornings, you can make Coffee Soup (another old-time favorite) to go along with your Hush Puppies. Simply tear bread into pieces and place in a bowl. Pour hot coffee over the bread, and add sugar and a bit of milk or cream to taste.

Hush Puppies

1 cup stone ground cornmeal
1 tsp. baking powder
½ tsp. salt
1 egg
½ cup milk (may need a bit more)
4 slices bacon

Mix together dry ingredients.

Beat together the egg and milk. Combine with dry ingredients and mix well. Cut up and fry bacon. Add cooked bacon to the rest of ingredients.

Fry hush puppies in bacon grease or vegetable oil until golden brown.

Serve with syrup or eat plain.

Oatmeal Muffins

1 cup rolled oats
1 cup milk
1 cup flour
⅓ cup sugar
1 T. baking powder
½ tsp. salt
1 egg, well beaten
¼ cup oil

Combine the oats and milk and let stand for 15 minutes.

In the meantime, sift together into a large bowl the flour, sugar, baking powder, and salt. Combine egg, oil, and oatmeal mixture. Add all at once to the dry ingredients and stir just until moistened.

Fill muffin tins ⅔ full and bake at 425° for 20-25 minutes.

Oatmeal Pancakes

2 cups rolled oats

2 cups buttermilk

½ cup unbleached white flour

½ cup whole wheat flour

2 tsp. sugar

1½ tsp. baking powder

1½ tsp. baking soda

1 tsp. salt

2 eggs

2 T. butter, melted and cooled slightly

These pancakes are started the night before. In a mixing bowl combine the oats and buttermilk. Cover and refrigerate overnight.

The next morning, in another mixing bowl, sift together the flours, sugar, baking powder and soda, and salt. Set aside.

In a large mixing bowl, whisk the eggs until they are light and frothy. Add the melted butter and mix together. Next, add the oatmeal/buttermilk mixture and mix well. Blend in the flour mixture; you will need to stir with a wooden spoon at this point because the mixture will be very thick. If it appears too dry, you can add a few more tablespoons of buttermilk.

Fry the pancakes in a small amount of vegetable oil, cooking well on both sides. These pancakes really puff up.

Serve them hot from the griddle with butter and maple syrup, but they are also excellent plain.

Notes:

BREAKFAST TREATS

Notes:

Peanut Butter Granola

1¼ cups honey

⅔ cup oil

1 cup peanut butter

1 T. salt

1 T. cinnamon

½ cup water

10 cups rolled oats

1 cup raw peanuts or other nuts, chopped

1 cup wheat germ

1 cup cornmeal

1 cup coconut

2 cups raisins

Combine the honey, oil, peanut butter, salt, cinnamon, and water in a saucepan and stir over low heat until peanut butter melts.

In a large bowl, combine the rolled oats, peanuts or other nuts, wheat germ, cornmeal, and coconut. Then add the peanut butter mixture and mix well.

Spread granola out in 2 large shallow greased pans and bake about 30 minutes at 325°, stirring often to prevent overbrowning, until crunchy and golden brown. When cool, add raisins.

Store in airtight container.

Poached Eggs

For a quick and easy breakfast, try good old-fashioned poached eggs on toast.

eggs

toast

In a shallow pan or skillet, bring water (about 1 inch deep) to a boil. Reduce heat slightly. Break each egg into a saucer and quickly slip the egg into boiling water. Cook, covered, 3 to 5 minutes. Lift the poached eggs out of the water with a slotted spoon. Drain them before putting them on buttered toast. Salt and pepper to taste.

Potato Crust Pie

2 cups potatoes, shredded (raw)
¼ cup onion, diced
½ cup bell pepper, diced (a combination of green and red bell peppers looks nice)
3 eggs
salt and pepper to taste
1 cup evaporated milk
½ tsp. paprika
½ tsp. salt
¼ tsp. pepper
1 cup cooked ham (leftovers work great), cubed in small pieces
1½ cups Cheddar cheese, shredded

Grease the bottom and sides of a 9-inch pie plate.

In a medium bowl, mix the potatoes, onion, bell pepper, 1 of the eggs (beaten), and salt and pepper to taste. Press potato mixture evenly over the bottom and up the sides of the prepared pie plate. Brush potato mixture with oil or melted butter and bake at 375° for 15 minutes.

Meanwhile, beat together the evaporated milk, remaining 2 eggs, paprika, salt, and pepper.

At the end of the first 15 minutes of baking, remove the crust from oven and layer the ham first and then the cheese. Pour the egg-and-milk mixture over the top of cheese and return pie to oven. Bake another 25-30 minutes, or until a toothpick inserted in the middle of the pie comes out clean. Let stand about 5 minutes before slicing and serving.

Notes:

BREAKFAST TREATS

Notes:

Potato Pancakes I

4 large potatoes, peeled, enough to measure 3 cups of grated potato

¼ cup onion, very finely chopped

2 eggs, slightly beaten

2 T. flour

¾ tsp. salt

pepper to taste

Grate potatoes using a large-sized grater. Pat dry.

In a large bowl, combine grated potato, onion, eggs, flour, salt, and pepper.

In a large, heavy skillet, slowly heat oil ⅛" deep until very hot but not smoking. Drop potato mixture into hot oil in 2-tablespoon increments. With a spatula, flatten pancakes against bottom of skillet. Fry 2 to 3 minutes on each side. Drain well on paper towels.

Potato Pancakes II

3 medium cooked potatoes, grated

1 egg, beaten

1 tsp. salt

In a medium bowl, mix all ingredients together.

Shape into patties and fry in greased skillet about 2-3 minutes on each side.

Potato Pancakes III

3 cups mashed potatoes
2 eggs, slightly beaten
¼ cup flour
5 T. milk
salt and pepper to taste

Mix together all ingredients and fry in a skillet well-greased with oil or a combination of oil and butter.

Notes:

This recipe is a great use for leftover mashed potatoes. You can make extra mashed potatoes for dinner so you have plenty of leftovers for breakfast in the morning.

Quick Cinnamon Breakfast Fans

3 cups flour
1 tsp. salt
4 tsp. baking powder
1 tsp. cream of tartar
⅓ cup sugar
¾ cup shortening
1 cup milk

Filling:
½ cup butter, melted
½ cup sugar
2 T. cinnamon

Stir together dry ingredients. Cut in shortening until the mixture is crumbled to the size of peas. Add milk and stir. Knead dough gently for ½ minute on a floured surface. Roll dough out in a rectangle about ¼-inch thick. (The rectangle should be about 8 x 24 inches.)

Spread over the top of the dough the melted butter, sugar, and cinnamon for the filling. Cut dough the long way into four 2-inch-wide strips. Then stack the four strips on top of each and cut the stack into 2-inch-wide pieces. Turn the pieces on their sides in a greased muffin tin so each treat fans out.

Bake at 400° for 12 minutes or until golden brown.

Notes:

This breakfast casserole gets put together the night before and refrigerated until morning.

Sausage and Egg Casserole

1 lb. bulk sausage
6 eggs
1 tsp. dry mustard
2 cups milk
1 tsp. salt
6 slices white bread, cubed
4 oz. mild cheese, cubed

Brown sausage and drain. Beat the eggs; add mustard, milk, and salt. Mix in the bread cubes, cheese, and sausage. Put in a buttered baking dish and refrigerate overnight.

In the morning, take the casserole out of the refrigerator and let set on the counter for a half hour while oven is preheating. Bake at 350° for 45 minutes. Remove from the oven and let set for several minutes before cutting.

Scrapple

1½ lb. ground pork
5 cups water, divided
1 tsp. salt
½ tsp. sage
1 cup cornmeal

Break up the ground pork into small pieces in a large saucepan. Add 4 cups of the water and stir, separating the pork well. Heat to boiling, reduce to simmer and cook 30 minutes. Remove meat from stock, reserve 3 cups of the stock, and add to it salt and sage.

Combine the cornmeal with 1 cup cold water (you can make part of this liquid milk, which will make the scrapple brown better when fried). Add this cornmeal/water mixture gradually to the hot stock; bring to a boil, reduce to simmer, cover, and cook 15 minutes. Stir in cooked ground pork. Pour into a loaf pan (9½ x 5 x 3-inches) and chill well for 24 hours. Slice ¼- to ½-inch thick. Fry pieces in hot oil quickly, turning only once. Allow room in the pan to turn. Serve hot either plain, with Tomato Gravy, or with syrup.

Stovetop Breakfast Casserole

1 T. butter
2 slices bread, torn up
½ lb. sausage, browned and drained
⅔ cup Cheddar cheese, shredded
½ cup fresh spinach, chopped
4 eggs
½ cup milk
salt and pepper to taste

Melt the butter in a skillet that has a lid and turn to cover the entire bottom of pan. Add torn bread and stir a bit to distribute evenly and completely cover the bottom of the pan. Sprinkle on sausage, cheese, and spinach.

Beat together the eggs and milk that have been seasoned with salt and pepper and pour over the sausage mixture. Cover and cook on medium-low heat for about 15 minutes or until eggs are set.

Tomato Gravy

¼ cup onion, diced small
2 T. bacon drippings
3 T. flour
1½ cups tomato juice or canned, stewed tomatoes including liquid, chopped fine
½ cup milk or light cream
2 tsp. brown sugar
salt and pepper to taste

Cook onion in bacon drippings until the onion is golden in color.

Add the flour and stir constantly for 30 seconds. Add the tomato juice or tomatoes and liquid in a steady stream, stirring constantly. Next add the milk or light cream and brown sugar and continue to stir until mixture thickens. Salt and pepper to taste.

Notes:

Tomato Gravy is great served over Scrapple, cornmeal mush, biscuits, or fried eggs and toast.

Notes:

Tomato Sour Cream Gravy

1 28-oz. can stewed tomatoes (or 1 quart home-canned)

½ cup sour cream

3 T. flour

1 tsp. sugar

¼ tsp. salt

¼ tsp. pepper

In a medium saucepan, cook the stewed tomatoes uncovered for about 10 minutes or until the liquid has been slightly reduced.

In a medium mixing bowl, whisk together the rest of the ingredients. Add about 1 cup of hot stewed tomatoes and mix well. Pour this mixture back into the hot tomatoes, stirring while adding, and cook until the mixture thickens.

Serve over cornmeal mush, Scrapple, or mashed potatoes.

Traditional Biscuits

2 cups flour

4 tsp. baking powder

½ tsp. salt

5 T. shortening

¾ cup milk

In a bowl, sift together the flour, baking powder, and salt. Cut the shortening into the flour mixture until it is completely incorporated. Make a well in the center and pour in the milk all at once. Stir with a fork until the dough comes clean from the sides of the bowl.

Turn the dough out onto a lightly floured surface and knead it gently about 10 times. Roll or pat to ½-inch thickness and cut the biscuits using a biscuit cutter or the top of a glass. Place biscuits on an ungreased baking sheet about 1 inch apart. Bake in a preheated 450° oven for 15-20 minutes.

Amish housewives grow many of the fruits and vegetables their families eat and preserve large quantities for the long winter months. Since few homes have refrigerators or freezers, the summer is busy with canning and drying. It's not uncommon for a woman to can as many as 2000 jars of food each summer.

BREADS, ROLLS, AND DOUGHNUTS

There is almost nothing better than the delicious scent of homemade bread rising and baking. Large Amish families eat many loaves of bread in a week, and it's not uncommon for as many as a dozen loaves to be baked at one time. Bread baking is an art form as much as a culinary skill, and Amish women take great care when baking their loaves, learning from their mothers how the dough feels when it has been kneaded long enough, how high to raise the dough, and the perfect oven temperature used to produce a loaf of bread that is high but doesn't fall, with small air pockets and a moist interior.

Bread baking takes some practice, but once the fundamentals are learned, it can be highly satisfying to add ingredients or tweak a recipe and make *your* bread a signature masterpiece. And before long you may find yourself making a number of loaves at a time, because once your family has a taste for warm bread fresh from the oven, they'll never want "boughten" bread again.

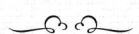

Give us this day our daily bread.
Matthew 6:11

Jesus said, "I am the bread of life."
John 6:48

Lord, in Your Word You teach us to ask for our daily bread so that we might be nourished and fed. Thank You, Father, that You daily meet the needs of my loved ones. And when I'm in the kitchen preparing meals for my family day in and day out (and especially on those days when I'm feeling a bit sorry for myself because the work seems endless and underappreciated), remind me that there is a deeper truth here: You are the Bread of Life, and You satisfy all our needs.

So as I go about my tasks, Lord, help me to put a smile on my face and a song in my heart, because when I'm honest with myself I realize there is no place on earth I'd rather be than here in this kitchen, with You right alongside me, preparing meals for those I love most.

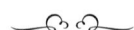

Amish Breakfast Puffs

1½ cups flour
1½ tsp. baking powder
½ tsp. salt
¼ tsp. mace
1 cup sugar, divided
⅓ cup oil
1 egg
1 tsp. vanilla
½ cup milk
6 T. melted butter
1 tsp. cinnamon

In a mixing bowl, combine flour, baking powder, salt, and mace.

In another mixing bowl, beat together ½ cup sugar, oil, egg, and vanilla on medium speed for 30 seconds. Add flour mixture and milk alternately to egg mixture, beating on low after each addition, just until combined.

Fill 10-12 greased muffin cups ⅔ full with batter. Bake at 350° for 15-20 minutes or until done.

Meanwhile, in a shallow bowl, place the melted butter. In another shallow bowl, combine the remaining ½ cup sugar and cinnamon.

When the puffs are done, remove from cups and, while still hot, roll the tops in melted butter and then in the cinnamon sugar. Serve immediately, either plain or with butter and jelly, if desired.

Bagels

4½ cups flour, approximately
4½ tsp. (2 packages) active dry yeast
1½ cups warm water
3 T. sugar
1 T. salt

In a large mixing bowl combine 1½ cups flour and yeast.

Notes:

All milk used in yeast bread recipes should be scalded and then cooled to lukewarm before using. Using milk instead of water usually gives a softer crust which becomes a richer brown when baked. When taking bread from the oven, grease the top with butter to make the crust softer.

In a separate bowl, combine the warm water, sugar, and salt; add to flour mixture. Beat at low speed for about 30 seconds, scraping sides of bowl constantly. Beat for 3 minutes on high speed.

Stir in as much of the remaining flour as you can mix in and then turn out onto a lightly floured surface. Knead while continuing to add enough flour to make a moderately stiff dough. Continue kneading until smooth and elastic; then cover and allow to rest for 15 minutes.

Cut dough into 12 portions; shape into smooth balls. Punch a hole in the middle of each with a floured finger. Pull gently to enlarge hole to about two inches across.

Place the bagels on a greased baking sheet; cover; and allow to rise for 20 minutes. Dip the bagels in the boiling water for about 10-15 seconds and put on a greased baking sheet.

Bake for 8-10 minutes at 350°; then broil for about 90 seconds on each side to brown.

Banana Nut Bread

⅔ cup sugar
⅓ cup shortening
2 eggs
3 T. sour milk or buttermilk
1 cup mashed bananas (slightly overripe bananas work best)
2 cups flour
1 tsp. baking powder
½ tsp. baking soda
½ tsp. salt
½ cup chopped walnuts

Mix together sugar, shortening, and eggs (an electric mixer works best). Stir in sour milk and mashed bananas.

Sift together the flour, baking powder, baking soda, and salt and blend into the banana mixture. Then add the walnuts.

Pour batter into a well-greased loaf pan. Let stand for 20 minutes before baking.

Bake at 350° for 50-60 minutes.

Basic White Bread

2¼ tsp. (1 package) active dry yeast
2 cups warm water
1 T. sugar
6 cups flour, approximately
1½ tsp. salt
2 T. softened butter

In a large mixing bowl, combine the yeast, water, and sugar; let stand until bubbly, about 10 minutes.

Combine 2 cups flour and the salt, add the yeast mixture, and beat at low speed. Add the butter. Turn to high speed and beat for 3 minutes. Add ½ cup flour and beat another 4 minutes.

Stir in another 2-3 cups flour, or enough to make a soft dough. Turn dough out onto a floured surface and knead for 8-10 minutes, adding just enough flour to make it workable, or until dough is smooth and elastic.

Place dough in a large buttered or oiled bowl, turning dough so all sides are greased. Cover with a clean towel and let rise until double, about an hour.

Punch down and knead again, then tear dough in half to make two balls of dough. Cover both with a clean towel and let stand for 20 minutes. Place dough into 2 loaf pans and cover and let rise in a warm place until double, about 45 minutes.

Bake at 400° for 25-30 minutes or until bread is done. Remove from oven and turn out onto a wire rack to cool. Immediately brush tops with melted butter if desired.

Notes:

BREADS, ROLLS, AND DOUGHNUTS

Notes:

Chocolate Baking Powder Doughnuts

2 cups flour
½ cup baking cocoa (unsweetened)
2½ tsp. baking powder
½ tsp. baking soda
¼ tsp. salt
¼ tsp. cinnamon
1½ T. butter, softened
¾ cup sugar
1 egg
½ cup milk

Sift together the flour, cocoa, baking powder, baking soda, salt, and cinnamon.

In a separate large mixing bowl, cream together the butter and sugar; beat in the egg and mix well. Alternately add flour mixture and milk, mixing well after each addition.

Turn out onto floured surface. Roll ¼-inch thick and cut into small doughnuts (2 inches or so in diameter).

Fry in oil, turning once, being careful not to crowd doughnuts while cooking. Drain on paper towels. When cool, sprinkle with powdered sugar or frost.

Chocolate Zucchini Bread

3 eggs, beaten
1 cup oil
1¾ cups sugar
1 T. vanilla
2 cups zucchini, grated
3 cups flour
1 tsp. salt
1 tsp. baking soda
1 tsp. baking powder
½ cup unsweetened cocoa
½ cup chopped nuts (optional)

In a large bowl, mix together the eggs, oil, sugar, and vanilla. Add the zucchini and stir.

In a separate bowl, mix together the flour, salt, baking soda, baking powder, and cocoa. Add dry ingredients to the zucchini mixture and blend well. Add nuts if using and stir again.

Grease and flour 2 loaf pans. Pour in batter. Bake at 350° for 45 minutes. Cool in pans for 10-15 minutes before removing zucchini bread to wire rack to finish cooling.

Notes:

The Amish are fond of tending large flower gardens but they do not cut flowers to enjoy indoors. They feel that God made flowers to be enjoyed where they grow, and cutting them shortens their life. However, they make use of potted plants inside their homes for decoration.

Notes:

For this recipe, I place the butter and evaporated milk in a small saucepan and gently warm them on the stove. Just be careful that the mixture doesn't get too hot.

Church Cinnamon Rolls

¾ cup sugar

⅓ cup butter, warmed

1 can evaporated milk, warmed

3 T. active dry yeast

3 eggs

4 cups flour (plus more as needed)

1 T. salt

¾ cup butter, softened

2-3 cups sugar

cinnamon

raisins and nuts, if desired

Put the ¾ cup sugar, ⅓ cup butter, evaporated milk, and yeast in a large stand mixer and let stand for 5 minutes. Then turn on mixer and mix these ingredients together. Add the eggs and, while mixing, slowly add the 4 cups flour and the salt. Continue adding flour until dough leaves the sides of the bowl. Continue kneading for 10 minutes and then place in a large, oiled bowl, cover with a towel, and let rise until doubled.

On a floured surface, roll out dough and spread with ¾ cup butter, 2-3 cups sugar, and lots of cinnamon. You can also spread on nuts or raisins, if desired.

Roll dough into a log and cut into 2 dozen rolls. Place cut side up on 2 greased jelly roll pans, cover with a towel, and let rise again.

Bake in a preheated 350° oven for 25 minutes or until done.

Communion Bread (Unleavened)

1½ cups flour

2 T. sugar

½ tsp. salt

½ cup butter

½ cup milk

In a large bowl, combine the flour, sugar, and salt. Cut in the butter using a pastry blender or two knives until it resembles coarse crumbs. Add the milk and mix until a stiff dough forms.

Turn out onto a floured surface and roll out very thin and uniform, about 17 x 13 inches. With a pizza cutter, even up the edges. Transfer the dough to a greased cookie sheet and cut into 1-inch-wide strips with the pizza cutter. Prick pieces with a fork about every inch.

Bake on a lower rack in the oven at 425° for 6 to 7 minutes. The outside strips may brown more quickly than the inside ones, so you can remove the outside strips and continue to bake the inner strips for a few minutes longer.

Break into 1-inch pieces to serve for communion, but if using for a meal, you can break off larger pieces.

Corn Bread

1 cup flour
1 cup cornmeal
¼ cup instant dry milk
2 T. sugar
4 tsp. baking powder
½ tsp. salt
1 egg
1 cup water
¼ cup oil

Grease a 9 x 9 x 2-inch pan.

In a mixing bowl, combine flour, cornmeal, instant milk, sugar, baking powder, and salt and stir to mix well.

In a medium sized bowl, beat egg and then add water and oil, beating until well blended. Stir into the cornmeal mixture. Beat by hand just until well blended and smooth. Pour batter into prepared pan.

Bake at 425° for 20 minutes.

Notes:

Dinner Rolls

2 T. sugar

2 T. shortening, melted and cooled

1½ tsp. salt

2¼ tsp. (1 package) active dry yeast

1 cup lukewarm water

3¼ cups flour

Add the sugar, shortening, salt, and yeast to the lukewarm water and let sit until bubbly, about 10 minutes. Add 1 cup of the flour and beat until smooth. Then by hand, mix in the remaining flour. Place the dough on a floured board and let it rest for about 5 minutes.

Knead the dough, adding small amounts of flour as needed, until smooth and elastic. Round into a ball and place the dough in a greased bowl, turning to grease all surfaces. Cover it and allow the dough to rise for 1 hour.

Pat out dough into a rectangle and roll up jelly roll style. (You can spread some softened butter on the dough before rolling it up if you want butter rolls.) Cut the log into 1-inch slices and place the rolls, cut side up, on a greased baking sheet.

Bake at 450° for 12-15 minutes.

The Amish use natural gas and propane to cook with, but wood-burning cookstoves are still common. Many of these old-fashioned cookstoves have a water reservoir that supplies hot water when needed. The Amish are known for their delicious sugar cookies, and when baked in a wood-burning cookstove, they come out light in color and softer than can be accomplished in a modern stove.

Easy Cinnamon Rolls

¾ cup milk

¾ cup water

½ cup shortening

½ cup sugar

2 eggs

2 tsp. salt

4½ tsp. (2 packages) active dry yeast, dissolved in ½ cup lukewarm water

7 cups flour, approximately

½ cup melted butter

cinnamon and sugar mixture

Sugar Glaze (recipe follows)

Heat milk and water together until scalded. Cool slightly.

Mix together shortening, sugar, eggs, and salt. Add milk and stir well. Add dissolved yeast and stir well. Add about half the flour and mix well. Turn out on a floured surface and add the remainder of the flour as needed while kneading until smooth, about 5 minutes.

Place dough in a large bowl, cover with a towel, and let rise till double in bulk, about 1 hour. Roll dough out to ¼-inch thickness. Cut with biscuit cutter. Roll each piece out so it's long and thin. Dip in melted butter and dredge in the cinnamon and sugar mixture. Roll each piece up and place in a baking pan, with their sides not quite touching. Let rise about 30-45 minutes, then place in a preheated 350° oven and bake until done, about 15 minutes. Can glaze with Sugar Glaze if desired.

Sugar Glaze

1½ cups powdered sugar

2-3 T. water

Mix together until well blended and to desired consistency. Drizzle over cooled cinnamon rolls.

Notes:

Adding a little sugar to the water used to dissolve the yeast will make the yeast more active. Your bread will turn out better.

Egg Bread

1½ cups scalded milk

½ cup butter

½ cup sugar

4½ tsp. (2 packages) active dry yeast

½ cup warm water

½ tsp. sugar

2 eggs, beaten

9 cups flour, more or less

2 tsp. salt

In a large mixing bowl, pour scalded milk over butter and sugar; cool.

In a small bowl, dissolve yeast in warm water with ½ tsp. sugar and let stand for 5 minutes.

Add the yeast mixture to the milk mixture and stir. Alternately add the eggs and three cups flour; then add the salt and beat for 3 minutes. By hand, continue adding the rest of the flour, and knead until the dough is light and elastic. Place the dough in a greased bowl and turn so all sides are covered. Cover and let rise until double.

Shape into 3 loaves and place in greased loaf pans. Let rise again for about 15 minutes.

Bake at 425° for 10 minutes and then turn down oven to 350° and continue baking for 30-40 minutes longer.

German Dark Rye Bread

3 cups regular flour

4½ tsp. (2 packages) active dry yeast

¼ cup baking cocoa powder

1 T. caraway seeds

2 cups water

⅓ cup molasses

2 T. butter

1 T. sugar

1 T. salt

3–3½ cups rye flour

In large mixing bowl combine regular flour, yeast, cocoa powder, and caraway seeds until well blended.

In a saucepan combine the water, molasses, butter, sugar, and salt; heat until just warm, stirring occasionally to melt butter. Add to dry mixture. Beat at low speed for 30 seconds and then turn to higher speed and beat for 3 minutes more.

By hand, stir in enough rye flour to make a soft dough. Turn out onto floured surface and knead until smooth, adding more rye flour as needed, about 5 minutes. Cover; let stand for 20 minutes.

Punch down and divide dough in half. Shape each half into a round loaf; place on greased baking sheets or 2 greased pie plates. Brush surface of loaves with a little cooking oil. Slash tops of loaves with a sharp knife. Let rise until double, about 45-60 minutes.

Bake at 400° for 25-30 minutes or until bread looks done. Remove from baking pans and cool on wire racks.

Notes:

Notes:

Ginger Pumpkin Bread

12 T. butter (1½ sticks), melted
1 15-oz. can pumpkin
3 eggs
2½ cups flour
2 tsp. baking powder
2 tsp. ground ginger
1 tsp. salt
1 cup sugar
1 cup brown sugar, packed
Sugar Glaze (recipe follows)

Whisk together the butter, pumpkin, and eggs.

Mix together the flour, baking powder, ginger, salt, sugar, and brown sugar and add to the pumpkin mixture until just combined. Do not overmix.

Divide batter between two greased loaf pans and bake at 375° for 50-55 minutes.

Cool for 10 minutes and then turn out on a rack to cool completely. Glaze with Sugar Glaze, if desired.

Sugar Glaze

1½ cups powdered sugar
2-3 T. water

Mix together until well blended and to desired consistency. Drizzle over cooled bread.

Graham Crackers

2 cups whole wheat flour
2 tsp. baking powder
¼ tsp. salt
4 T. brown sugar
½ cup butter
2 T. honey
2 T. milk
dash of vanilla
cinnamon sugar

Mix together all ingredients to make dough. Turn out onto a cookie sheet and roll out. Sprinkle surface with cinnamon sugar and lightly press sugar mixture into surface of dough. Deeply score dough in squares. Bake at 375° for 8 minutes. Allow to cool slightly before cutting through crackers.

Herb Biscuits

2 cups flour
2 tsp. baking powder
¼ tsp. baking soda
1 tsp. salt
¼ tsp. dry mustard
½ tsp. sage
½ tsp. celery seed
¼ cup shortening
¾ cup buttermilk

Mix together the dry ingredients and herbs. Cut in the shortening; add liquid and stir to make a soft dough. Knead lightly about 20 times. Roll or pat out ½-inch thick. Cut into biscuits and place on an ungreased cookie sheet.

Bake at 425° for 10 minutes or until golden brown and done.

Notes:

TIPS FOR A SUCCESSFUL GARDEN

Root vegetables, such as potatoes and onions, should be planted when the moon is waning. This assures the gardener that the vegetables won't spend their energy on the plant tops. Vegetables that grow above ground, such as squash, peas, beans, and tomatoes, should be planted when the moon is waxing, which will ensure a bountiful harvest.

The best time to plant corn is when the new leaves on oak trees are the size of squirrels' ears.

To avoid dirty fingernails, before you go outside to plant or weed, run your fingernails through a bar of soap. It will keep the dirt out and make washing up after easier.

Protect your smaller garden tools from

Honey Oatmeal Bread

1 cup boiling water
1 cup rolled oats, uncooked
⅓ cup shortening, softened
⅓ cup honey
1 T. salt
4½ tsp. (2 packages) active dry yeast
1 cup warm water
1 egg
4-5 cups wheat flour

Stir the boiling water, oats, shortening, honey, and salt together in a large mixing bowl. Cool to lukewarm.

Dissolve yeast in warm water.

Add dissolved yeast mixture, egg, and 2 cups flour to the first mixture. Beat 2 minutes at medium speed, or by hand, until batter is smooth. By hand, gradually stir in remaining flour to make a stiff batter. Spread batter evenly in two greased loaf pans. Smooth tops of loaves by patting into shape. Cover and let rise in warm place about 1½ hours. Bake at 375° for 50-55 minutes. Remove bread from pans and brush tops with melted butter.

Long Johns

4½ tsp. (2 packages) active dry yeast
4 cups flour (may need ½ cup or so more)
¼ cup sugar
1 tsp. salt
½ tsp. nutmeg
½ cup water
½ cup half-and-half
¼ cup shortening
1 egg
oil for deep frying
Maple Frosting (recipe follows)

In a large mixing bowl, combine yeast, 1½ cups of the flour, sugar, salt, and nutmeg; mix well.

In a saucepan, heat together the water, half-and-half, and shortening until warm but not hot; shortening will not be entirely melted. Add to the flour mixture. Add egg and blend at low speed until moistened, and then beat at medium speed for 3 minutes.

By hand, gradually stir in enough remaining flour to make a soft dough. Turn out onto a floured surface and knead until smooth and elastic, 5-8 minutes. Place in a greased bowl and turn to grease all surfaces. Cover and let rise until double, about 1 hour.

Punch down dough and divide into 2 parts. Roll or pat out each piece to a 12 x 6-inch rectangle. Cut into 1-inch strips (each piece will be 6 inches long by 1 inch wide). Cover and let rise until double, about 30 minutes.

Heat oil to 425° and fry until golden brown. Drain on paper towels and when cool, frost with Maple Frosting (recipe follows).

Notes:

continued

rusting by keeping a pail of sand near the garage or cellar door and plunging them into the sand when through with them.

To make flowers grow better, soak eggshells in warm water overnight. Remove the shells and use the water to water your flowers.

Plant marigolds in your vegetable patch to help keep away bugs and rabbits.

Put some wood ashes on the ground where you plant radishes to keep the worms away.

Notes:

You can tell how hard a winter it will be by how many layers onions grow; the more layers, the harder the winter.

Maple Frosting

½ cup brown sugar, packed
¼ cup butter
¼ tsp. maple flavoring
2 T. half-and-half
1 cup powdered sugar

In a small saucepan, mix together the brown sugar and butter. Heat, stirring constantly to boiling; boil for 2 minutes, continuing to stir constantly. Remove from heat and immediately stir in maple flavoring and half-and-half. Stir in enough powdered sugar until the frosting has a spreadable consistency.

Oatmeal Bread

2 cups milk
2 cups rolled oats, uncooked
¼ cup brown sugar, packed
2 T. shortening
1 T. salt
2¼ tsp. (1 package) active dry yeast
½ cup warm water
5 cups flour, approximately
egg white (see directions)
1 T. water
small amount rolled oats

Scald milk; stir in 2 cups oats, brown sugar, shortening, and salt. Remove from heat and cool to lukewarm.

In large mixing bowl, sprinkle yeast on water and stir to dissolve. Add milk mixture and 2 cups flour to yeast. Beat with a spoon until batter is smooth. Add enough remaining flour, a little at a time, until dough becomes soft and leaves the sides of the bowl. Turn onto a floured board and knead until dough is smooth and elastic, about 8 minutes.

Place the dough ball in a lightly greased bowl. Turn to allow the dough to become greased on all sides. Let stand in a warm place, covered, until doubled, about 1 hour. Punch down and let rise again until nearly double, about 30 minutes.

Turn onto board and divide in half. Make 2 balls. Cover and let rest for 10 minutes. Shape into loaves and place in 2 greased loaf pans. Let rise again until almost doubled, about 1 hour. Brush the top of the loaves with egg white beaten with 1 tablespoon of water (optional). Sprinkle top with rolled oats.

Bake at 375° for 40 minutes or until done. If bread starts getting too brown, cover loosely with aluminum foil after at least 15 minutes of baking time.

Oven-Baked Doughnuts

4½ tsp. (2 packages) active dry yeast
¼ cup warm water
1½ cups milk, scalded and then cooled
½ cup sugar
1 tsp. salt
1 tsp. nutmeg
¼ tsp. cinnamon
2 eggs
⅓ cup shortening
4½ cups flour
¼ cup butter, melted
cinnamon sugar or plain sugar

In a large mixing bowl, dissolve the yeast in the warm water. Add the milk, sugar, salt, nutmeg, cinnamon, eggs, shortening, and 2 cups of the flour. Beat these ingredients with an electric blender for ½ minute, scraping the sides of the bowl often. Stir in the remaining flour and mix until the batter is smooth. Cover and let rise in a warm place until double, about 1 hour.

Turn the dough out onto a well-floured board, and roll the dough around in the flour so all surfaces are covered. The dough will be soft to handle. With a flour-covered rolling pin, gently roll the dough to ½-inch thickness. With a floured biscuit or doughnut cutter, cut out doughnuts and lift them carefully with

Notes:

a spatula and place on a greased baking sheet, 2 inches apart. Brush them with melted butter and let them rise until double, about 20 minutes.

Bake the donuts at 425° for 8-10 minutes or until they are golden brown. Remove from oven and immediately brush them with melted butter and shake on cinnamon sugar.

Peasant Bread

2¼ tsp. (1 package) active dry yeast

1 T. sugar

2 tsp. salt

2 cups warm water

1 T. oil, plus more for brushing top of loaf (olive oil tastes great in this recipe)

4½ cups flour

Mix together the yeast, sugar, and salt; add the warm water and mix together; add oil. Begin adding the flour, incorporating well after each addition; knead the dough until smooth, about 5-7 minutes. Place dough in a greased bowl and cover. Let rise for 30 minutes.

Form into a round loaf and place on a greased cookie sheet. Cover and let rise again, about 45 minutes.

Brush top of loaf with oil and bake in a preheated 425° oven for 10 minutes; reduce heat to 375°, brush again with oil, and continue baking for 20 more minutes.

Pluck-Its

Pluck-Its

⅓ cup sugar

⅓ cup butter, melted

½ tsp. salt

1 cup milk, scalded

2¼ tsp. (1 package) active dry yeast

¼ cup warm water

3 eggs, beaten

4 cups flour

Coating

1 cup sugar

3 T. cinnamon

½ cup nuts, chopped fine

½ cup butter, melted

Add sugar, butter, and salt to scalded milk. Dissolve yeast in warm water. When milk is lukewarm, add the yeast and water mixture, eggs, and flour. Beat thoroughly. Cover and let rise until double.

In a small bowl, mix together the sugar, cinnamon, and nuts. Put the melted butter in a separate bowl. Take a teaspoon of the dough, roll into a ball, and dip it into the melted butter and then into the sugar-and-cinnamon mixture, being careful to coat the entire ball.

Pile the coated balls of dough loosely into an ungreased angel food cake pan. Let rise 30 minutes and then bake in a preheated 350° oven for 35 to 40 minutes or until done. Immediately turn the pan upside down onto a serving platter.

Notes:

Bread is better when worked down at least two times; three is even better if time permits. For a finer textured bread, try letting the dough rise in a place where it is a little cooler so it takes longer to rise. The little bubbles of trapped air in the dough will be smaller and the bread will not be as crumbly. Also, if the bread is baked before the last rising is completely doubled, the texture of the finished product will be softer and less crumbly.

Notes:

Pumpkin Bread

3 cups brown sugar
5 cups wheat flour
1 tsp. cinnamon
½ tsp. cloves
1 tsp. salt
1 T. baking soda (be generous)
1 cup oil
2½ cups canned pumpkin
2 eggs

Mix together all ingredients, starting with the dry ones. When thoroughly blended, divide between two greased loaf pans.

Bake at 350° for about 1 hour and 20 minutes or until done.

Pumpkin Cinnamon Rolls with Caramel Frosting

⅓ cup milk
2 T. butter
½ cup canned pumpkin or mashed cooked pumpkin
2 T. sugar
½ tsp. salt
1 egg, beaten
2¼ tsp. (1 package) active dry yeast
1 cup flour
1 cup bread flour
⅓ cup brown sugar, packed
1 tsp. cinnamon
2 T. melted butter
Caramel Frosting (recipe follows)

In small saucepan, heat milk and 2 T. butter just until warm and butter is almost melted, stirring constantly.

In large mixing bowl, combine pumpkin, sugar, and salt. Add milk mixture and beat with electric mixer until well mixed. Beat in egg and yeast.

In a separate mixing bowl, combine flours. Add half of flour mixture to the pumpkin mixture. Beat mixture on low speed for 5 minutes, scraping sides of bowl frequently. Add remaining flour and mix thoroughly. Dough will be very soft. Turn into lightly greased bowl; lightly butter or grease surface of dough. Cover and let rise in warm place until doubled, about 1 hour.

Punch down the dough and then turn it onto a floured surface and knead a few turns until it is smooth, sprinkling with enough additional flour to make the dough easy to handle. On a lightly floured surface, roll dough into a 12 x 10-inch rectangle.

In a small bowl, combine brown sugar and cinnamon. Brush surface of dough with melted butter and then sprinkle with brown sugar mixture. Beginning with long side, roll up dough jelly roll style. Pinch seam to seal. With a sharp knife, cut into 12 1-inch slices. Place rolls, cut side up, in a greased 9-inch square baking pan. Cover and let rise until nearly doubled, about 30-45 minutes.

Bake rolls at 350° about 20 minutes or until done. Remove from pan to a wax paper-lined wire rack and cool for 10 to 15 minutes before frosting.

Caramel Frosting
¼ cup butter
½ cup brown sugar, packed
2 T. milk
¼ tsp. vanilla
dash of salt
½ to ¾ cup powdered sugar, sifted to break up any lumps

In a small saucepan, heat butter until melted. Stir in brown sugar and milk. Cook over medium-low heat for 1 minute. Transfer to small mixing bowl and cool mixture. Stir in vanilla, salt, and ½ cup powdered sugar. Beat with electric mixer until well blended. If necessary, add more powdered sugar for desired consistency.

Notes:

Quick and Easy Pizza Crust

1 cup warm water
4½ tsp. (2 packages) active dry yeast
1 tsp. sugar
1 tsp. basil
¼ tsp. garlic powder
½ tsp. salt
2½ cups flour, approximately

Combine water, yeast, and sugar. Let sit 5 minutes. Add rest of ingredients and mix into dough. Turn the dough onto a floured surface and knead until smooth, about 5-7 minutes. Let rest for 20 minutes.

Grease a pizza pan or cookie sheet and press out dough to fit the pan.

Bake for 7 minutes at 400°. Take out and top with pizza sauce and your favorite toppings and return to the oven to bake an additional 8-12 minutes or until done.

Refrigerator Dinner Rolls

2¼ tsp. (1 package) active dry yeast
2 T. warm water
1 cup very hot water
1 tsp. salt
6 T. shortening
¼ cup sugar
1 egg, well beaten
3½ cups flour

In a small bowl, combine yeast with warm water and set aside until light and bubbly, about 10 minutes.

In a large mixing bowl, combine the hot water, salt, shortening, and sugar and mix well. Cool to lukewarm. Add the yeast mixture, stir, and then add the beaten egg and half of the flour; beat well.

With a wooden spoon (and then with your hands, if necessary) stir in more of the flour, enough to make the dough easy to handle. Grease the top of the dough, cover, and store in the refrigerator for up to one week.

When you want to bake the dinner rolls, take out the amount of dough needed. Shape into balls and put on a greased baking pan or in muffin tins. Cover and let rise in a warm place until dough warms up and doubles in bulk, about 1½ hours.

Bake at 425° for 12-15 minutes.

Soda Crackers

¼ cup lukewarm water
4½ tsp. (2 packages) active dry yeast
1 tsp. baking soda
2 T. warm water
8 cups flour, approximately
1 T. salt
1¾ cups water
⅔ cup oil or melted shortening

In a small bowl (preferably not metal) mix together the ¼ cup lukewarm water and yeast. Set aside until bubbly, about 10 minutes.

In another small bowl, mix together the baking soda and 2 tablespoons warm water. Set aside.

In a large bowl, mix together 4 cups flour, salt, 1¾ cups water, oil or melted shortening, baking soda mixture, and yeast mixture. Mix until well blended. Add about 4 cups more flour and turn out dough and knead for approximately 10 minutes, adding flour as needed.

Divide dough into several small portions. Roll dough ⅛-inch thick and cut into squares. Prick with a fork.

Bake at 350° for 10 minutes or until lightly browned.

Notes:

Notes:

Soft Pretzels

4½ tsp. (2 packages) active dry yeast
¾ cup warm water
¼ tsp. salt
4 T. brown sugar
1 cup flour
1½ cups bread flour
1 cup water
4 tsp. baking soda
1 egg, beaten with 1 tsp. water
coarse salt

Dissolve yeast in the warm water and let stand for 5 minutes. Add the salt, brown sugar, and flours and mix well. Knead, adding small amount of additional flour as needed so the dough doesn't stick, for about 4-5 minutes. Return to bowl, cover, and let rise for 15-20 minutes. Do not punch down. Divide dough into 8 pieces and shape into large pretzels.

Dip pretzels into a soda water mixture of 1 cup water and 4 tsp. baking soda and place on paper towels for a minute before putting them on a greased cookie sheet. Brush pretzels with egg-and-water mixture and then sprinkle with coarse salt.

Bake at 450° for 12-15 minutes or until golden brown.

Sourdough Bread

½ cup Sourdough Starter, room temperature (recipe follows)
1 cup lukewarm water
4 cups flour, divided
1 tsp. sugar
1 tsp. salt
2-3 T. cornmeal
Boiling water
1 egg white, beaten

Early in the morning, make the sponge by mixing together in a large bowl the Sourdough Starter, lukewarm water, and 2 cups flour. Mix thoroughly. Cover with plastic wrap and let stand in warm area for at least 8 hours. (You can also begin this the night before, let stand overnight, and bake the bread in the morning.)

Add sugar and salt to sponge and mix well. Gradually mix in remaining flour. Turn dough out onto lightly floured surface and knead until smooth and elastic, about 5-10 minutes. Transfer dough to a greased bowl, turning to coat all surfaces. Cover with plastic wrap and let stand in a warm area until double in size, about 1-1½ hours.

Sprinkle a baking sheet with cornmeal. Punch dough down and shape into a 12-inch long loaf. Transfer to baking sheet. Cover with plastic wrap and let stand until double, about 1 hour.

Position rack in center of oven and preheat oven to 400°. Fill a pie plate or cake pan with boiling water and set on bottom shelf of oven. Make 3 slashes diagonally across top of loaf using the tip of a sharp knife.

Brush loaf with some of the beaten egg white. Bake for 10 minutes. Brush top of loaf again with the egg white and continue baking for about 20-30 minutes. Remove from oven, transfer to wire rack, and cool some before slicing.

Sourdough Starter

2 cups warm water
4½ tsp. (2 packages) active dry yeast
2 cups flour

Do not use a metal bowl.

Dissolve yeast in water and let set until bubbly, about 10 minutes. Stir in flour. Let set at room temperature, covered, at least 2 days before using. Stir occasionally. To store, stir it down and put into a jar. Cover and keep in the refrigerator. In order to keep starter a long time, it's necessary to replace some of the starter with fresh. You can do this by taking out 1 cup starter and replenishing with 1 cup flour and 1 cup water; mix and let stand until bubbly, cover, and store in refrigerator.

Notes:

The longer you keep feeding and using your Sourdough Starter, the more "sour" the taste will become.

Notes:

For Sourdough Starter, see p. 61.

Sourdough English Muffins

2¼ tsp. (1 package) active dry yeast
½ cup warm water
3 cups flour, approximately
1 cup Sourdough Starter, room temperature
2 T. oil
1 T. sugar
1 tsp. salt
cornmeal

In a large mixing bowl, dissolve yeast in warm water. Let stand until bubbly, about 10 minutes. Add 2 cups flour, Sourdough Starter, oil, sugar, and salt. By hand, stir until smooth. Gradually stir in enough remaining flour to make a firm dough.

Turn out onto floured surface and knead until smooth and elastic, about 5 minutes. Place in a greased bowl, turning to grease all surfaces. Cover and let rise until doubled, about 1 hour.

Punch down dough; let rest about 5 minutes. On a surface that has been sprinkled with cornmeal, roll out dough to ¼-inch thickness. With a round biscuit cutter, cut into circles and turn to coat top side with cornmeal.

Place on a greased cookie sheet, cover, and let rise until double, about 30 minutes.

With your hands, carefully lift the English muffins from the cookie sheet and place in a lightly greased griddle or frying pan. Cook for 10 minutes on each side or until deep golden brown.

Sourdough Pancakes

½ cup Sourdough Starter, room temperature

1¼ cups flour

1 cup milk

1 T. sugar

1 T. oil

1 tsp. soda

½ tsp. salt

1 egg

In a large mixing bowl, combine the starter, flour, and milk. Let stand for 30 minutes.

By hand, stir in remaining ingredients; the batter will be slightly lumpy.

Pour a small amount of batter onto a lightly greased griddle or frying pan. Cook until golden, turning to cook the other side when the surface is bubbly and edges look slightly dry.

Sourdough Rye Bread

1 cup Sourdough Starter, room temperature

1 cup warm water

2 cups rye flour

1 T. active dry yeast

1 cup warm water

1 T. salt

1 T. caraway seeds

1½ tsp. poppy seeds

2 cups whole wheat flour

2 cups white flour

cornmeal

1 egg, beaten

1 tsp. water

Mix the Sourdough Starter, 1 cup warm water, and rye flour together and let stand overnight.

Notes:

For Sourdough Starter, see p. 61.

Notes:

The next day, mix the yeast and 1 cup warm water and let stand until bubbly, about 10 minutes. Stir the yeast mixture into the starter mixture and add the salt, caraway and poppy seeds, and both remaining flours. Add more white flour if needed to make a workable dough. Knead for about 10 minutes. Let rise until doubled.

Punch down the dough and knead about 10 times. Form the dough into 2 long loaves. Put them on a baking sheet that has been sprinkled with cornmeal. Let rise until double. Brush loaves with beaten egg mixed with 1 tsp. water.

Preheat oven to 450°. Turn down oven to 350° and immediately put in the loaves. Bake for 45 minutes. Turn loaves over and continue to bake another 10 minutes to brown the bottom slightly.

Sticky Buns

⅓ cup milk
¼ cup sugar
½ tsp. salt
¼ cup butter
2¼ tsp. (1 package) active dry yeast
¼ cup warm water
1 egg
2½ cups flour

Filling

½ cup butter, softened and divided
1 cup light brown sugar, divided
½ cup chopped walnuts
½ cup chopped raisins
½ tsp. cinnamon

In a small saucepan, heat milk just until bubbles form around edge of pan. Remove from heat and add sugar, salt, and ¼ cup butter. Stir to melt the butter. Cool to lukewarm.

Sprinkle yeast over warm water in a large mixing bowl and stir to dissolve. Stir in lukewarm milk mixture. Add the egg and 2 cups of flour and mix until smooth. Add the remaining ½ cup flour and hand mix until dough is smooth and leaves the sides of the bowl.

Turn out dough onto a floured surface and continue to knead the dough until it is smooth and blisters appear, about 7 minutes. Place dough in an oiled bowl, turning the ball of dough over so oiled side of dough is now up. Cover with a towel and let rise in a warm place until doubled—about 1-1½ hours.

Meanwhile, make the filling. In a small bowl, cream together ¼ cup butter with ½ cup brown sugar. Spread this mixture on the bottom and sides of a 9 x 9 x 2-inch square baking pan. Sprinkle with walnuts.

Roll dough into a 16 x 12-inch rectangle and spread with remaining butter. Sprinkle with remaining brown sugar, the raisins, and cinnamon. Roll up from long side jelly roll fashion and pinch long edge to seal. Cut cross-wise into 12 pieces and place, cut sides down, in prepared pan. Cover with a towel and let rise until doubled, about 1 hour.

Bake in a preheated 375° oven for 25 to 30 minutes. Remove from oven, invert on a cookie sheet or other larger pan for 1 minute, and then remove baking pan.

Notes:

Notes:

Sweet Cream Buns

1½ cups milk
¼ cup sugar
2¼ tsp. salt
¾ cup shortening
¾ cup lukewarm water
1 T. sugar
6¾ tsp. (3 packages) active dry yeast
3 eggs, beaten
7 cups flour

Cream Filling

¼ cup shortening
½ cup milk
3 cups powdered sugar
1 tsp. vanilla

Scald the milk and then add sugar, salt, and ¾ cup shortening. Stir to dissolve; cool to lukewarm.

In a large mixing bowl, stir together lukewarm water and 1 T. sugar to dissolve the sugar. Sprinkle in yeast and let stand for 10 minutes. Beat with fork. Stir yeast mixture into the milk mixture. Add the beaten eggs. Stir in 4 cups flour and beat until smooth and elastic. Work in 3 cups flour; turn out onto a floured surface and knead lightly until smooth, about 5 minutes, adding small amounts of flour as needed. Place dough in a buttered bowl and turn so all sides are greased. Cover and let rise in a warm place until double, about 1½ hours. Shape dough into approximately 48 balls and place in large, buttered baking pans. Let rise till double and then bake at 375° for 25 minutes or until done. Immediately after removing the buns from the oven, brush the tops with melted butter.

Just before serving, make the cream filling. Beat the shortening, milk, powdered sugar, and vanilla together until light and fluffy. Slit the buns and fill with the sweet cream filling. Replace tops and serve.

Sweet Johnny Cake

1 egg, beaten
1 cup sour cream
1 tsp. baking powder
1 tsp. baking soda
½ cup flour
¾ tsp. salt
1 cup sugar
1½ cups cornmeal

Stir together the egg and sour cream. Mix in the dry ingredients and pour into a loaf pan or small square baking dish. Bake at 350° for 30 minutes or until golden brown on top. Serve with maple syrup and warm milk.

Walnut Bread with Streusel Filling

3 cups flour, sifted
1 cup sugar
4 tsp. baking powder
2 tsp. salt
1 egg, slightly beaten
¼ cup shortening, melted
1½ cups milk
1 tsp. vanilla
1½ cups chopped walnuts
Streusel Filling (recipe follows)

Sift together the flour, sugar, baking powder, and salt. Add egg, shortening, milk, and vanilla and stir just until all the flour is moistened. Stir in walnuts.

Pour half of batter into a greased 9 x 5 x 3-inch loaf pan. Sprinkle with Streusel Filling; top with remaining batter and bake at 350° for about 1 hour and 20 minutes or until done.

Notes:

Notes:

Streusel Filling

⅓ cup brown sugar, packed

1½ T. flour

1 tsp. cinnamon

2 T. butter

Mix all ingredients together, breaking up butter until mixture resembles coarse peas.

Wheat Bread

2¼ tsp. (1 package) active dry yeast

2 cups lukewarm water

2 T. sugar

2 tsp. salt

3 cups white flour

½ cup hot water

⅓ cup brown sugar

2 T. shortening

1 T. oil

3 cups whole wheat flour

In a large mixing bowl (do not use metal) mix yeast and lukewarm water and allow to stand for 10 minutes. Add sugar, salt, and white flour. Beat with a wooden spoon or mixer until smooth. Set in warm place until light and bubbly.

Meanwhile, combine hot water with brown sugar, shortening, and oil; cool to lukewarm. Add to sponge and mix well with wooden spoon. Add whole wheat flour and mix. Turn out onto a floured surface and knead, adding enough flour so it doesn't stick, for about 5-7 minutes. The dough should be smooth and elastic. Cover and let rise until doubled (about 1 hour). Divide into 2 greased loaf pans and let rise until dough reaches the top of the pan (don't let it rise too high or it will fall during baking).

Bake at 375° for 35-40 minutes or until done.

To clean brass bottoms on cooking pots, rub catsup on a soft cloth and polish until the brass shines. Then rinse and dry.

Wheat Bread (Large Batch)

4 cups hot (not boiling) water
1 cup powdered milk
1 cup honey
2-3 heaping T. active dry yeast
2 T. salt (scant)
1 cup oil
4 cups wheat flour
12 cups white flour, approximately

In a large bowl (do not use metal) mix together the water, milk, honey, yeast, salt, and oil. Let stand for 10 minutes.

Add the wheat flour and mix well. Begin adding the white flour and when the dough leaves the sides of the bowl and you can no longer mix with a spoon, turn out dough onto a floured surface and continue adding the flour as you knead. Knead for 5-7 minutes.

Cover and let rise until doubled, about 1 hour. Divide into 4 greased loaf pans and let rise slightly in pans before baking.

Bake at 350° for 30-40 minutes or until done.

Wheat Muffins

1 cup whole wheat flour
1 cup white flour
1 tsp. baking soda
¼ tsp. salt
3 T. melted shortening or butter
¼ cup brown sugar
1 cup buttermilk
1 egg

Mix together the flours, baking soda, and salt.

Mix together the shortening or butter, brown sugar, buttermilk, and egg; add to flour mixture. Mix just until blended.

Pour batter into greased muffin tins and bake at 350° for 15-20 minutes.

Notes:

Whole Wheat Crackers

2 cups whole wheat flour

1 tsp. salt

½ cup sesame seeds

¼ cup wheat germ

¼ cup oil

¼ cup Parmesan cheese

½ cup water (slightly more if needed)

Mix together all ingredients. Add enough water to hold dough together. Roll out on a floured board (thinner dough makes crisper crackers) and cut into desired shapes.

Bake on an ungreased cookie sheet at 350° for 8-10 minutes.

Whole Wheat Quick Buttermilk Bread

1 quart buttermilk

4 cups whole wheat flour

3 cups brown sugar

pinch of salt

1 tsp. baking soda

Mix together all ingredients and pour batter into 2 greased loaf pans. Bake at 350° for 60-70 minutes.

This recipe is about as easy as it gets. But try it once and you'll want to make it again and again. Delicious!

Zucchini Bread

3 cups flour
1½ cups sugar
1 tsp. cinnamon
1 tsp. salt
1 tsp. baking powder
1 tsp. baking soda
2 cups zucchini, shredded
1 cup nuts, chopped
1 cup raisins
3 eggs, beaten
1 cup oil
cinnamon sugar

In a large bowl, stir together the dry ingredients. Add the zucchini, nuts, and raisins. Mix together the eggs and oil and pour over the dry ingredients. Stir until blended.

Pour into two loaf pans or a bundt cake pan, sprinkle with cinnamon sugar, and bake at 350° for 40-45 minutes or until done.

Zwieback

2 cups milk
1 cup shortening
2 tsp. salt
4 T. sugar, plus 2 tsp., divided
1 cup warm water
2¼ tsp. (1 package) active dry yeast
2 eggs, beaten
8-10 cups flour

Scald the milk and then add the shortening, salt, and 4 T. sugar. Cool slightly.

In a small bowl stir to dissolve 2 tsp. sugar in warm water. Sprinkle yeast over the top, stir, and let stand until bubbly, about 10 minutes.

Notes:

Add yeast mixture and beaten eggs to warm milk mixture. Mix well and gradually stir in flour. Turn out onto a lightly floured surface and knead dough until very soft and smooth, using as little flour as possible. Cover and let rise in a warm place until double in bulk.

Pinch off small balls of dough the size of a small egg. Place balls 1 inch apart on a greased cookie sheet. Put a smaller ball of dough on top of the first one and press with your thumb to create an indent. Let rise again until double, about 1 hour.

Brush with beaten egg white if desired and bake at 400° for 15-20 minutes.

SOUPS AND STEWS

The Amish believe that children are a "heritage from the Lord," and it's not uncommon to see families with ten or more children. That's a lot of hungry mouths to feed, and a steaming bowl of hot soup or hearty stew will help satisfy the hunger of growing bodies. These dishes are healthy, tasty, and economical too, and they will be found often at Amish tables, especially during the colder winter months. In summer, fruit soup is enjoyed at mealtime—often the fruit used in the soup come evening is whatever was processed in the kitchen that day.

When you eat the labor of your hands,
you shall be happy, and it shall be well with you.

Psalm 128:2

Lord, I am so glad I'm a keeper of my home! You have set in my heart the desire to nurture my loved ones and I am grateful. When I am in the kitchen, kneading dough for bread or cutting up vegetables for a savory soup or stew, my mind often turns to thoughts of You.

I praise Your holy name, Lord, and I am reminded anew of Your love for me—Your child.

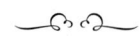

Amish Bacon Bean Soup

1 pound bacon ends or sliced bacon, cut into small pieces
1 pound navy beans
1 chopped onion
4 quarts water, approximately
salt and pepper to taste

Place all ingredients in a large pot and simmer for at least 2 hours or until beans are thoroughly cooked.

Amish Church Soup

1 onion, chopped
½ stick butter
3 cups cooked navy beans
4 quarts milk
bread, cut in bite-sized pieces
salt and pepper to taste

Brown chopped onion in butter. Add beans and milk. Bring just to the boiling point. Add bread cubes and salt and pepper to taste.

Amish Egg Soup

2 T. butter
¼ cup water
3 quarts milk
salt
pepper
allspice
2 quarts stale bread, cubed
6 hard-boiled eggs, chunked

Melt butter in a large saucepan; add water and bring to the boiling point before adding the milk. Add salt, pepper, and allspice to taste. Bring the mixture just to the boiling point and then remove from heat. Add the bread cubes and eggs and let stand for several minutes while bread softens and soup thickens.

Notes:

Bacon ends are inexpensive and have lots of smoke flavor and meat.

This recipe will serve 15 people.

Notes:

Baked Beef Stew

¼ cup flour

¼ tsp. celery seed

1¼ tsp. salt

⅛ tsp. pepper

2 pounds beef, cut into bite-sized cubes

4 small onions, sliced

5 potatoes, thinly sliced

2 carrots, sliced

4 tsp. beef bouillon

1 tsp. Worcestershire sauce

1½ cups hot water

Mix together the flour and seasonings and dredge the beef chunks in the mixture. In a large casserole dish with a tight-fitting lid, arrange layers of meat and vegetables. Add the bouillon and Worcestershire sauce to the hot water and stir to mix. Pour evenly over the stew.

Cover the casserole dish and bake at 325° for 3 hours, checking occasionally to make sure it doesn't cook dry. If so, add a little very hot water.

Beef and Barley Soup

½ lb. hamburger

1 cup carrots, peeled and finely diced

1 stalk celery, finely diced

¼ cup onion, finely diced

½ cup pearl barley

2 quarts beef broth

salt and pepper to taste

Brown hamburger and drain off fat. Combine all ingredients and cook, covered, until barley is tender, about 1 hour.

Broccoli and Cottage Cheese Soup

1 cup celery, diced
1 cup onion, diced
3 cups broccoli, chopped
1 cup cottage cheese
1 can cream of chicken soup
2 cups milk
½ tsp. salt
⅛ tsp. pepper

Cook celery, onion, and broccoli in a small amount of water until tender; do not drain.

Blend together the cottage cheese and soup until smooth. Add milk and mix well. Add to undrained vegetables and heat but do not boil.

Cabbage Chowder

3 cups water
4 cups cabbage, coarsely shredded
2 cups carrots, sliced
3 cups potatoes, diced
1 T. salt
½ tsp. sugar
¼ tsp. pepper
4 cups scalded milk
2 T. butter

Cook the vegetables and seasonings until tender in enough water to barely cover them; add a bit of water if necessary while cooking to keep them covered. Add the scalded milk and butter and heat thoroughly without boiling.

Notes:

Notes:

Chicken Chowder

2 T. butter

¼ onion, chopped

1½ cups cooked chicken, cubed

1½ cups potatoes, peeled and cubed

1½ cups carrots, peeled and sliced

2 cups chicken broth (or use 2 cups water and 2 chicken bouillon cubes)

1 tsp. salt

1 tsp. pepper

3 T. flour

2½ cups milk

⅛ cup fresh parsley, chopped

Melt the butter in a saucepan. Add onion and sauté until tender. Add chicken, potatoes, carrots, broth (or water and bouillon), salt, and pepper. Cover and simmer 20 minutes or until vegetables are tender.

Combine flour and ½ cup milk in a jar and cover and shake until blended. Add flour and milk mixture to the soup and stir until blended. Add remaining milk. Stirring constantly, continue to cook until mixture thickens. Stir in parsley and serve.

Chunky Beef Vegetable Soup to Feed a Hundred

2½ gallons water
4 large onions, chopped
8 quarts carrots, peeled and diced
6 quarts peas
8 quarts potatoes, peeled and diced
4 quarts green beans
1 quart celery, diced
½ cup salt (or to taste)
⅛ cup pepper
20 lbs. hamburger
5 quarts beef broth
8 quarts tomato juice
4 cups brown sugar
4 T. Kitchen Bouquet seasoning sauce
4 quarts cooked roast beef, cut into bite-sized pieces
cornstarch

In a very large pot, combine the water, vegetables, and salt and pepper and bring to a boil. Simmer until the vegetables are cooked and tender. Drain off the water.

Meanwhile, in a large pot or in a smaller pot in batches, brown the hamburger. Drain off most of the fat, but keep some to help flavor the soup.

When the vegetables have been cooked and drained and returned to the very large pot, add the beef broth, tomato juice, brown sugar, Kitchen Bouquet, hamburger (including the reserved grease), and roast beef. Let soup simmer to enhance the flavors. You can adjust the seasoning at this time.

You can also thicken the soup by adding some cornstarch that has been mixed with cold water. Gradually stir in the cornstarch and water, stirring constantly while the soup thickens.

This makes about 60 quarts of soup and can be canned in quart jars following instructions from a good guide (such as the *Ball Blue Book;* see Resources section).

Notes:

Triumph is just a little "try" and a lot of "umph."

Notes:

WEATHER LORE

A thick husk on the corn in the field means a long, cold winter ahead. If the ears protrude from the husk, the coming winter will be short and mild.

If the brown stripes on "wooly bears" are broad, a cold winter is ahead.

If a dog's fur grows thick in the fall, the winter will be cold.

A halo around the moon or sun means rain will arrive within 3 days.

If cows lie down in the field, expect rain soon. If they stay standing, it will be a light shower.

Snow is God's fertilizer—it covers plants and protects them, helping to keep nutrients from washing away, as they do with the rain. Frost is God's plough because it breaks up the ground and kills pests.

Coffee Beef Stew

1 cup flour
1½ tsp. salt
½ tsp. pepper
1 tsp. thyme
3 lb. stew beef, cubed
3 T. oil
5 cups beef broth or stock
1 cup strong brewed coffee
1 T. Worcestershire sauce
1 tsp. paprika
1 tsp. sugar
3 T. catsup
6 potatoes, peeled and quartered
2 onions (or 1 large), quartered
6 carrots, peeled and quartered
½ cup peas, fresh or frozen

Place the flour, salt, pepper, and thyme in a bag and shake to blend. Add the beef cubes, a few at a time, and shake to coat.

In a large stockpot, heat the oil until hot and add the beef cubes; brown on all sides. Next, add the rest of the ingredients except for the peas. Reduce heat to low, cover, and simmer for 2 hours. Add the peas and continue cooking for another 15-30 minutes.

Corn Chowder

1 onion, finely chopped

2 stalks celery, finely chopped

4 T. butter

4 cups chicken broth

4 potatoes, peeled and cut in bite-sized pieces

2 tsp. salt

1 tsp. pepper

1 clove garlic, minced

1 T. parsley, minced

2 quarts frozen (thawed) or fresh corn

1 cup top milk or half-and-half

3 cups milk

In a large pot, sauté onion and celery in the butter until onions are translucent. Add the chicken broth, potatoes, salt, pepper, and minced garlic and parsley and simmer for 30 minutes. Add corn and simmer gently for another 15 minutes or so. Add the top milk or half-and-half and regular milk and heat thoroughly.

Cream of Cabbage Soup

½ lb. bacon, coarsely chopped

12 cups cabbage, shredded

1 onion, chopped

2½ quarts chicken broth

1 cup half-and-half

2 tsp. salt

½ tsp. pepper

Swiss cheese, shredded, for garnish

In a large pot, fry the bacon until crisp; do not drain. Remove bacon and set aside. To the bacon drippings in the pot, add the cabbage and onion and sauté for 10 minutes, stirring occasionally, until cabbage is limp but not browned. Add the chicken broth and simmer until the cabbage and onions are tender, about 15 minutes. Add the half-and-half, salt, and pepper and heat through but do not boil.

When serving, sprinkle soup with bacon and cheese.

Notes:

Easy Hamburger Stew

½ lb. hamburger
1 small onion, chopped
1 quart green beans
6 potatoes, peeled and cubed
2 quarts beef broth
salt and pepper to taste

Brown the hamburger and drain off the fat. Add the rest of the ingredients and simmer until potatoes are tender.

Farmer's Favorite Soup

1 lb. hamburger
1 large onion, chopped
1 cup celery, chopped
1 large potato, peeled and diced (at least 1 cup)
1 cup carrots, peeled and sliced
salt and pepper to taste
1 cup tomato sauce
2½ quarts water
¼ cup cornmeal
¼ cup water

Brown meat and onion and drain off fat. In a Dutch oven or heavy soup pot, add the meat and onion mixture, celery, potatoes, carrots, salt and pepper, tomato sauce, and 2½ quarts water. Simmer, covered, until vegetables are tender.

Make a thin paste of the cornmeal and ¼ cup water. Add to the soup, stirring as you do so it doesn't lump up. Continue stirring until slightly thickened, about 2 minutes.

Five-Hour Beef Stew

2 lb. beef stew meat, cubed

3 onions, chopped

6 carrots, chopped

1 cup celery, chopped

1 package frozen peas

1 can (#2 can) tomatoes

2 T. tapioca

½ T. sugar

1 T. salt

1 slice stale bread, torn

4 potatoes, peeled and cubed

Mix all ingredients together. Place in a covered 2½ quart (or larger) casserole dish. Bake at 250° for 5 hours.

Fruit Soup

2 quarts cold milk

¾ cup brown sugar

1 tsp. vanilla

4 cups fresh fruit, cut into bite-sized pieces

bread cut into bite-sized pieces

Mix together the milk, sugar, and vanilla. Place bread cubes and some fruit pieces into individual serving bowls and ladle the milk mixture over top.

Notes:

This soup is especially good on a hot summer day.

Notes:

Hasenpfeffer Stew

1 rabbit, dressed and cut into pieces

1-2 cups water

flour for dredging

1 tsp. salt

¼ tsp. pepper

¼ cup fat (such as bacon) or oil

2 onions, sliced

2 cloves garlic, minced

½ cup vinegar

1 can stewed tomatoes

1 small can tomato paste

½ tsp. cloves

Cook rabbit pieces in 1-2 cups water in a covered stockpot or Dutch oven until meat can easily be deboned. Strain broth and save to add to stew. When cool enough to handle, debone meat and cut into pieces.

Roll pieces of meat in flour and sprinkle with salt and pepper. Fry in fat or oil until browned. Remove and set aside. Add the onion to the fat and cook until limp and slightly browned. Add back the meat and broth, and then add all other ingredients. Cover and let simmer, or bake at 350°, for 1-1½ hours.

Knepp Soup

2 cups flour

2 tsp. baking powder

½ tsp. celery salt

½ cup milk

1 egg

2 T. butter, melted

6 cups beef or chicken broth

In a large mixing bowl, whisk together the flour, baking powder, and celery salt. Whisk together the milk, egg, and melted butter until well mixed. Make a well in the flour mixture and pour the milk mixture into it. Stir until a stiff dough forms, but add a bit more milk if dough looks too dry. Cut the dough in half and let stand, covered, for 10 minutes.

Heat the broth to boiling in a wide pan. You want to have enough liquid surface to hold all the knepps at the same time.

Tear or cut the dough into small pieces (no bigger than an inch). Gradually add the knepps to the boiling broth. Cover, reduce heat, and cook for 12-15 minutes. Do not lift the lid during cooking.

Lentil Soup

5 cups broth or water (beef broth tastes especially good)
1 cup lentils
1 onion, chopped
2 stalks celery, chopped
2 carrots, peeled and chopped
1 clove garlic, minced
1 large potato, diced
2 cups canned tomato sauce
½ tsp. curry powder
½ tsp. basil
salt and pepper to taste

Combine all the ingredients in a large pot and simmer for 1-2 hours.

Notes:

Notes:

Meatball Chowder

2 lb. hamburger

2 tsp. salt

⅛ tsp. pepper

2 eggs, beaten

¼ cup chopped fresh parsley

½ cup crushed cracker crumbs or bread crumbs

2 T. milk

5 T. flour

4 small onions, chopped

2 cups celery, diced

4 cups potatoes, peeled and diced

¼ cup rice

6 cups tomato juice or V-8 juice

6 cups water

1 T. sugar

1 tsp. salt

1½ cups frozen corn, or a mixture of frozen corn and peas

Combine the hamburger, salt, pepper, eggs, parsley, crumbs, and milk. Mix thoroughly with your hands and then form into balls the size of walnuts. Dredge meatballs in the flour and fry in a large pot to which you have added some oil so they don't stick while browning. When meatballs have browned, add all the remaining ingredients except the corn. Bring the mixture to a boil, reduce heat, cover with a tight-fitting lid, and continue to cook until vegetables are tender. Add the corn last and cook for 10 more minutes.

Meatball Stew

1½ lb. hamburger

1 egg

1 cup bread crumbs or oatmeal

½ cup onion, diced

salt and pepper to taste

2 T. shortening

2 cans tomato soup

2 cans beef broth

2 cans water

¼ tsp. thyme

4 potatoes, cubed

4 carrots, sliced

Mix together the meat, egg, bread crumbs or oatmeal, onion, and salt and pepper. Roll into meatballs and brown in shortening. Drain. Add tomato soup, beef broth, and cans of water. Next, add the thyme, potatoes, and carrots. Simmer until vegetables are tender, about 1 hour.

Notes:

Notes:

To quickly and easily chop nuts, place between two layers of waxed paper and roll with a rolling pin.

Mennonite Stew

2 T. oil
3 lb. stewing beef
2 cups onion, chopped
3 T. flour
2 cups water
1 tomato, chopped
5 potatoes, peeled and cubed
4 carrots, peeled and sliced
½ tsp. thyme
½ tsp. rosemary
1 tsp. salt
1 tsp. pepper
1 cup peas, frozen or fresh
½ bell pepper, diced

Heat oil in a large pot and brown beef and onions. Sprinkle flour to coat meat and stir, cooking for 1 minute. Add water and tomato, cover, and simmer on low heat for 2 hours. Add more water if stew looks dry.

Add potatoes, carrots, and spices; cover and simmer another hour.

Add peas and bell pepper and simmer an additional 15 minutes.

Potato Rivvel Soup

3 lb. potatoes, peeled and cubed
½ cup onion
pinch of salt
2 T. butter
salt and pepper
1 cup milk
1 cup water
rivvels (recipe follows)

Put potatoes and onions in a large kettle with water to barely cover and a pinch of salt and cook until the potatoes are done.

Do not drain the water. Take a potato masher and mash the potatoes in the water until they are roughly mashed. There will still be small lumps. Then add the butter and salt and pepper to taste.

Next, add the liquid—you need to use a combination of milk and water because the milk gives the soup a creamy richness. Bring the soup to a gentle bubbling simmer. Make the *rivvels*.

Rivvels

1 cup flour
½ tsp. salt
1 egg

In a medium bowl, mix the flour and salt. Break the egg into the flour mixture and mix together until you have lumps about the size of grapes. This is a fairly messy process, so feel free to use your hands to mix. Drop these *rivvels* into the soup and, stirring occasionally, cook them until done, about 10 minutes or so depending on their size. If the soup is too thick, you can add more milk. Adjust the seasoning to taste before serving.

Notes:

Rivvels can be put in any boiling liquid. A batch of rivvels cooked in a pot of chicken or beef broth, or even warm milk, makes a great addition to lunch or dinner. Add some vegetables and pieces of meat, serve it with fresh-baked bread or biscuits, and you have a complete meal.

Shipwreck Stew

1½ lb. hamburger, browned and drained
1 large onion, diced
1 quart potatoes, cooked and diced
1 pint carrots, cooked and diced
8 oz. egg noodles, cooked
1 pint peas
1 can cream of chicken soup
1 can cream of celery soup
1 can cream of mushroom soup
Velveeta cheese slices

Layer in the order given (except the Velveeta) in a casserole dish and bake at 350° for 1 hour. Slice Velveeta cheese as thin as you can and lay over the top of the casserole. Return to the oven to continue baking until the cheese is melted and bubbly.

Notes:

This is a dry stew. You can also cook this all day on low in a Crock-Pot, but add about 2 T. water or broth to the pot.

Stonaflesch

2 lb. hamburger
10 carrots, peeled and sliced
6 large potatoes, peeled and thinly sliced
salt and pepper
paprika

In a heavy oven-proof pot, layer a portion of the hamburger (raw) with some of the carrots and then potatoes. When each layer has been completed, salt and pepper and then continue layering. It's better to have several thin layers versus just a few thick ones. Be sure to end with a small amount of hamburger. Sprinkle paprika over the top and cover with a tight-fitting lid.

Bake at 350° for at least an hour, or until carrots and potatoes are cooked through and tender. If you have the time, bake it at 250° for 3-4 hours, being careful not to scorch the bottom.

Tramp Soup

10 medium potatoes, peeled and diced
¼ cup onion, chopped
milk
1 lb. cooked ham chunks or country smoked sausage
3 T. flour
1 cup milk
½ lb. Velveeta cheese, cut into small cubes

Boil the potatoes and onions together until just tender. Pour off most of the water, return the potatoes and onions to the pot, and add milk to barely cover. Add the meat and heat until simmering. Meanwhile, put the flour and 1 cup of milk into a jar and shake well. When the soup starts to bubble, and while stirring constantly, gradually add the flour and milk mixture. Stir for several minutes until slightly thickened. Turn the heat to very low, add the Velveeta cheese, and let set for 5 to 10 minutes, stirring occasionally, until the cheese is melted.

Vegetable Stew

½ head cauliflower, cut into small pieces

2 potatoes, peeled and diced

2 carrots, thinly sliced

½ eggplant, cut into small pieces

4 tomatoes, skinned, seeded, and chopped

2 onions, thinly sliced

2 zucchini, thinly sliced

2 yellow crookneck squash, thinly sliced

½ cup fresh green peas (can use frozen also)

½ cup fresh green beans

1 bell pepper, chopped

2 celery stalks, chopped

salt and pepper to taste

½ cup fresh dill, chopped

½ cup fresh parsley, chopped

1½ cups beef or chicken broth

½ cup olive oil

In a large greased roasting pan, arrange a third of the vegetables in a single layer. Sprinkle with some of the salt, pepper, dill, and parsley. Repeat layers two more times.

In a small saucepan, heat together the broth and oil. Pour over the vegetables, cover the roaster tightly with aluminum foil or a lid, and bake at 350° for 3 hours or until vegetables are tender.

White Bean Soup

1 lb. white beans (navy or northerns)

2½ quarts water—enough water to cover beans

1 ham hock (you can also use pieces of ham or several bacon slices)

2 stalks celery

1 onion, chopped

Put the beans in a large soup pot and add the water. Turn the heat on, and when the water begins to boil, turn the heat off,

Notes:

cover the pot, and let sit for an hour. Drain water off the beans and then refill pot with fresh water and return beans to the stove. Once they begin to boil, turn down the heat so the beans simmer. At that point you can add the ham hock or other meat, celery, and onion.

Simmer, covered, for 2 or more hours, stirring occasionally, until the beans are tender. Remove hock from soup and take off any meat to add back into pot. Salt and pepper to taste. When serving, you can ladle the bean soup over cornbread or a bit of rice and add chopped tomatoes or eat it plain.

SALADS AND DRESSINGS

Salads are often made using ingredients from the family garden, but the Amish are also fond of Jell-O salads for special occasions, and hearty potato and macaroni salads that can feed many. In early spring Amish children will forage for dandelion greens to make a tasty salad that is rumored to cleanse the blood, which has turned sluggish from the long winter.

*Better is a little with righteousness,
than vast revenues without justice.
Pleasant words are like a honeycomb,
sweetness to the soul and health to the bones.*

PROVERBS 16:8,24

Lord, sometimes I believe the adage "a woman's work is never done." It seems that no matter how hard I work, there is always more that needs doing. But may I never get so involved in the cares and chores of the day that I forfeit the best thing in life, which is to love my family with all my heart. May I always be quick to kiss away "owies," wipe away tears, referee squabbles, and show my family in countless small ways how much I love them. Lord, You died for each of them, and they are worth my best efforts. Thank You for my family!

Basic Oil and Vinegar Salad Dressing

1 cup oil
½ cup vinegar (experiment with different vinegars, such as cider or balsamic)
Salt and pepper to taste

Put ingredients in a jar and shake to blend. The dressing will separate, but just shake again right before using.

Beet and Apple Salad

2 cups cooked beets, cooled and diced
2 cups raw apples, diced
2 hard-boiled eggs, chopped
½ cup mayonnaise
¼ cup walnuts

Combine all ingredients and toss lightly. Serve on a bed of lettuce.

Carrot and Pineapple Salad

1 package (3 oz.) orange Jell-O
1 cup boiling water
1 cup pineapple juice
1 cup crushed pineapple (canned)
1½ cups carrots, shredded

Dissolve the Jell-O in boiling water and then add pineapple juice. Chill. When the Jell-O begins to set, add the pineapple and carrots. Pour the mixture into a mold and chill until set. Unmold on lettuce leaves. Serve with mayonnaise.

Notes:

God gives us the ingredients for our daily bread, but He expects us to do the baking.

Notes:

Chicken Salad

3 cups cooked chicken, diced
½ cup celery, diced
1 cup mandarin oranges, drained
1 cup pineapple tidbits, drained
½ cup grapes, cut in half
¼ cup mayonnaise
¼ cup sour cream
½ tsp. lemon juice
1 tsp. sugar

Combine chicken, celery, mandarin oranges, pineapple, and grapes. Mix together mayonnaise, sour cream, lemon juice, and sugar; pour over chicken mixture, toss gently, and chill. Serve on a bed of lettuce.

Coleslaw

1 medium cabbage
½ tsp. salt
2 eggs
1 T. butter
1 cup sugar
½ cup vinegar
½ cup cream

Shred or slice cabbage fine. In a double boiler, add all other ingredients except cream. Cook until thick, being careful not to scorch. Cool to room temperature (or refrigerate) and then add cream. Pour dressing over cabbage.

Cottage Cheese Salad

2 boxes (3 oz. each) Jell-O (any flavor)
2 cups boiling water
1 cup cream, whipped
1 cup miniature marshmallows
1 small can crushed pineapple, drained
2 cups cottage cheese

Mix together the Jell-O and boiling water and stir until Jell-O is dissolved. Set in the refrigerator until slightly thickened and then add the remainder of the ingredients. Chill until set.

Cream Dressing

½ cup heavy whipping cream
4 T. lemon juice
4 T. sugar
salt and pepper to taste

Combine the ingredients and either shake in a jar or whisk until well blended and sugar is dissolved. Use this as a dressing for spinach or lettuce salad.

Creamy Pea Salad

1 cup cooked peas, drained and cooled
1 cup celery, finely diced
½ cup sweet pickles, finely diced
½ cup Cheddar cheese, chopped in bite-sized pieces
mayonnaise
salt and pepper to taste

Mix together all ingredients and add mayonnaise until you have reached a desired creaminess. Salt and pepper to taste.

Notes:

Creamy Ribbon Salad

First layer

1 package (3 oz.) cherry Jell-O

Prepare according to package directions and pour into a rectangular glass pan. Chill until set.

Second layer

⅔ cup milk
16 marshmallows
1 package (8 oz.) cream cheese
1 package (3 oz.) lemon Jell-O
1 small can crushed pineapple
⅔ cup walnuts, chopped
1 cup whipping cream, whipped

Heat the milk, marshmallows, and cream cheese in a double boiler until melted, and then add the Jell-O. Stir until dissolved. Let mixture cool before adding the pineapple, nuts, and whipped cream. Pour over the first layer and chill until set.

Third layer

1 package (3 oz.) orange Jell-O

Prepare Jell-O according to package directions and pour over the other layers. Chill until set.

Dutch Slaw

1 large cabbage, chopped

½ cup vinegar

1 cup celery, diced

2 tsp. salt

½ tsp. mustard seeds

½ cup onion, diced

2 cups sugar

1 green pepper, diced

1 tsp. celery seeds

Mix together all ingredients and put them in a large glass bowl or jar. Cover tightly and refrigerate. This slaw will last a long while if kept refrigerated.

French Dressing

½ cup oil

½ cup catsup

2 T. lemon juice

2 T. vinegar

1 T. onion, grated

1 tsp. salt

2 T. sugar

1 tsp. paprika

Combine all ingredients and shake in a jar until well blended.

Notes:

Notes:

Fruit Salad Poppy Seed Dressing

⅓ cup honey
1 tsp. salt
2 T. vinegar
1 T. prepared mustard
¾ cup oil
1 T. onion, minced
1 T. poppy seeds

Combine honey, salt, vinegar, and mustard. Gradually add the oil, whisking while adding. Continue whisking until well blended. Add the onion and poppy seed. Cover and chill for several hours so the flavors have a chance to blend.

Fruit Salad with Dressing

Fruit Salad

4 apples, pared, peeled, and cut into bite-sized pieces
4 oranges, peeled, sectioned, and cut into pieces
½ fresh pineapple, cut into pieces
2 cups strawberries, hulled and cut into pieces
3 bananas, cut into pieces
1 small bag pecans

Mix together all salad ingredients and set aside.

Dressing

½ cup sugar
¼ cup lemon juice
1 egg, beaten with a fork
1 cup whipping cream, whipped, but not stiff

Cook the sugar, lemon juice, and egg until thickened, about 5 minutes. Cool thoroughly. Fold mixture into the whipped cream, and then mix into the fruit.

German Potato Salad

8 potatoes, peeled, cubed, and boiled
1 stalk celery, chopped
2 hard-boiled eggs
1 onion, chopped
1 T. fresh parsley, minced

Combine all ingredients in a large bowl and then prepare dressing.

Dressing

4 slices bacon, diced
2 eggs, well beaten
1 cup sugar
½ cup vinegar
½ cup cold water
¼ tsp. dry mustard
½ tsp. salt
¼ tsp. pepper

Fry the bacon in a skillet until crisp. Remove the bacon bits and add to salad. Beat together eggs, sugar, vinegar, water, and spices. Pour mixture into the hot bacon grease and cook, stirring, until mixture thickens, about 10 minutes. Pour over the potato mixture and mix lightly. Refrigerate for several hours before serving.

Honey Dressing

½ cup oil
½ cup honey
½ cup vinegar
1 tsp. salt

Combine all ingredients and shake in a jar until well blended.

Notes:

Notes:

Try a dash of kindness with a pinch of love today. Top it off with a bit of cheerfulness and add a touch of goodwill. Your day will be much better for it.

Hot Chicken Salad

2 cups cooked chicken, diced
2 cups celery, chopped
2 T. onion, finely diced
½ cup almonds, slivered
½ cup mild Cheddar cheese, grated
½ tsp. salt
1 tsp. lemon juice
1 cup mayonnaise (or ½ cup each mayonnaise and sour cream)
½ tsp. prepared mustard
1 cup potato chips, coarsely crushed

Combine the chicken, celery, onion, almonds, cheese, and salt. In a separate bowl, mix together the lemon juice, mayonnaise, and mustard; pour over chicken mixture and toss gently. Put in a lightly buttered casserole dish, sprinkle with potato chips, and bake at 375° for 15-20 minutes.

Serve with French bread or crackers, or allow to cool slightly and spoon onto a bed of lettuce.

Layered Salad

1 head of lettuce, torn into pieces
1 cup celery, diced
4 hard-boiled eggs, diced
3 cups peas, cooked
½ cup bell pepper, diced
1 medium sweet onion, diced
8 slices bacon, cooked, cooled, and torn into small pieces
2 cups mayonnaise
2 T. sugar
4 oz. Cheddar cheese, grated

Using a 9 x 12-inch dish, layer the first 7 ingredients. Mix the mayonnaise and sugar together until well blended and then spread over the top of the other ingredients, as if you are frosting a cake. Go all the way to the edges, being careful to seal all edges. Sprinkle on the grated cheese. Set in refrigerator for 8-12 hours. At serving time, you can garnish with some fresh parsley and more bacon pieces if desired.

Macaroni Salad

3 cups chilled cooked macaroni (about 1½ cups uncooked)
2 slices crisp cooked bacon, torn into pieces
1 cup celery, chopped
2 T. onion, minced fine
2 T. fresh parsley, minced fine
¼ cup bell pepper, finely diced
salt and pepper to taste
mayonnaise to taste
milk or half-and-half to taste
hard-boiled eggs for garnish

Combine all ingredients in a bowl and toss together with mayonnaise mixed with a little milk or half-and-half. Adjust seasonings and put in a serving bowl. Garnish with hard-boiled eggs, if desired.

Our Molded Jell-O Salad

1 small package (3 oz.) lime Jell-O
1¾ cups liquid (from pineapple tidbits and hot water)
1 small package cream cheese
1 T. vinegar
2 T. sugar
1 small can pineapple tidbits
⅓ cup chopped nuts
¼ pint cream, whipped

Dissolve Jell-O in 1 cup hot water; add remaining liquid to complete 1¾ liquid total (drain off pineapple juice and use as part of liquid). Add cream cheese and beat on low with an

Notes:

"Our Molded Jell-O Salad" might sound like an odd name, but the recipe originally came from my grandmother, and that's what she called it. This salad is more like dessert and always popular with the youngsters. When Thanksgiving or Christmas comes around, I can count on at least one of my boys asking, "Mom, you're going to make our molded Jell-O salad, right?" A funny name for a delicious dish.

Notes:

Just one pound of seed potatoes can yield 20 pounds of potatoes in the garden, and they are so easy to grow. Simply hold back a few of the potatoes you buy to feed your family—the ones that have developed eyes are best—and in the spring cut them into several pieces (you want at least one eye per piece), plant them about 4 inches deep, water, and watch them grow. They are ready to dig and either cure or eat fresh when the leaves of the plants begin to die back. Home-grown potatoes are so good. The skin is tender, and they taste sweeter than store-bought ones.

electric mixer until frothy and cheese is broken up completely. Add vinegar, sugar, pineapple, and nuts and stir completely. Pour into your favorite Jell-O mold or bowl and set in the refrigerator until it begins to set. Then fold in the whipped cream and chill for several hours until set.

Plain and Tasty Potato Salad

5 lbs. potatoes, peeled, cubed into bite-sized pieces, and boiled
6-8 eggs, hard-boiled
1 cup onion, finely diced
1 cup celery, chopped
¼ cup dill pickles, chopped very fine
3 cups mayonnaise (plus a little more)
3 T. prepared mustard
salt and pepper to taste
paprika

When the potatoes are cooked, drain the water off and then cool them quickly. You can run fresh, cold water over them, or set the colander in a sink filled with ice cubes.

Once the potatoes are cool, put them in a very large container and add the remainder of the ingredients except for one hard-boiled egg and the paprika, and mix together until well blended. Start with about 2 cups mayonnaise and keep adding mayonnaise until the potato salad is the consistency you like.

Put the potato salad into a large serving bowl. Thinly slice the remaining hard boiled egg and use the slices and a sprinkle of paprika to decorate the top.

Rhubarb Salad

3 cups rhubarb, chopped
½ cup sugar
¼ tsp. salt
⅓ cup water
2 packages (3 oz. each) strawberry Jell-O
1 cup celery, finely diced
2¼ cups water
1 T. lemon juice
½ cup chopped nuts

Heat thoroughly the rhubarb, sugar, salt, and water until rhubarb is somewhat soft. Then add the rest of the ingredients and refrigerate until set.

7-Up Salad

2 boxes (3 oz. each) lemon Jell-O
2 cups boiling water
2 cups 7-Up
2 bananas, sliced
1 cup crushed pineapple, drained, reserving liquid

Topping

½ cup sugar
3 T. flour
1 egg, beaten
1 cup pineapple juice
2 T. butter
1 cup cream, whipped

Dissolve Jell-O in boiling water and then add 7-Up. Chill until partly set and then add the bananas and pineapple.

For the topping, whisk together the sugar, flour, egg, and pineapple juice. Bring to a boil, stirring over medium heat. When thickened, remove from heat and add the butter. Cool, stirring occasionally, and then add the whipped cream and gently mix together. Spread over the Jell-O.

Notes:

The discovery of a new dish does more for the happiness of man than the discovery of a star.

Notes:

Sauerkraut Salad

1 large jar or can kraut, undrained
1 cup onion, chopped
1 cup celery, chopped
1 cup green bell pepper, chopped
1½ cups sugar
½ cup oil
½ cup vinegar

Combine all ingredients in a large nonmetallic bowl and soak overnight in the refrigerator. When ready to serve, drain off the liquid and place in a serving dish.

Sour Cream Cucumber Slices

2 large cucumbers, peeled and thinly sliced
1 small onion, sliced and separated into rings
½ cup sour cream
1 T. lemon juice
1 T. sugar
salt and pepper to taste

Combine the cucumber and onion in a medium-sized bowl. Add the remaining ingredients and toss lightly to mix. Chill at least 2 hours before serving to blend the flavors.

Sour Cream Dressing

1 cup sour cream

2 T. vinegar

½ tsp. salt

1 T. lemon juice

1 T. green onion, finely minced

3 T. sugar

Combine the ingredients and shake in a jar until blended. Chill well before using.

Strawberry Pretzel Salad

1 cup pretzels, coarsely crushed

½ cup sugar

¾ cup butter, softened

⅓ cup chopped nuts

1 8-oz. package cream cheese

1 cup sugar

1 cup whipping cream, whipped

1 6-oz. box strawberry Jell-O

2 cups boiling water

2 10-oz. boxes frozen strawberries (approximately 2½-3 cups)

Mix together the crushed pretzels, ½ cup sugar, butter, and nuts. Press the mixture lightly into a greased rectangular glass baking dish. Bake 10 minutes in a 350° oven. Cool.

Combine the cream cheese, 1 cup sugar, and whipped cream. Spread on the cooled pretzel layer and refrigerate.

Dissolve the Jell-O in the boiling water. Add the frozen strawberries. When 75 percent set, put on top of the cream cheese layer. Refrigerate for several hours or overnight.

Notes:

Notes:

Summer Salad

2 cups fresh spinach, washed and dried
1 cucumber, peeled and thinly sliced
4 green onions, chopped
½ cup radishes, thinly sliced
2 cups cottage cheese
paprika to taste
1 cup sour cream
2 tsp. lemon juice
½ tsp. salt
¼ tsp. pepper
½ cup fresh parsley, minced

Chop the spinach, add the cucumber, onions, and radishes, and toss lightly. Arrange in a large salad bowl and place the cottage cheese in a mound in the middle. Sprinkle the cottage cheese with paprika.

Blend the sour cream with the lemon juice, salt, and pepper and pour over the salad. Toss when ready to serve and sprinkle the parsley over the top.

Sweet Potato Salad

3 lb. sweet potatoes, cooked, peeled, and cubed
½ cup onion, finely chopped
1 cup green pepper, chopped
1½ cups mayonnaise
salt to taste
¼ tsp. pepper
dash of hot pepper sauce

Combine all the ingredients except mayonnaise, salt, pepper, and hot sauce. Add these ingredients together and mix well. Add to sweet potatoes, cover, and refrigerate for several hours before serving.

Tangy Marinated Bean Salad

1 can (16 oz.) green beans, drained
1 can (15½ oz.) garbanzo beans, drained
1 can (15 oz.) kidney beans, drained
½ onion, minced fine
1 cup celery, minced fine
1 tsp. salt
½ cup vinegar
¼ cup oil

Mix the beans together and then add the rest of the ingredients and mix well. Marinate this salad overnight before serving.

Thousand Island Dressing

1 cup mayonnaise
½ cup sweet pickle relish, drained
¼ cup catsup
2 green onions, minced fine
salt and pepper to taste

Blend together all ingredients. Put in a container with a tight-fitting lid and store in refrigerator.

Triple-Layer Salad

First layer

1 package (3 oz.) strawberry Jell-O
2 bananas

Prepare the Jell-O according to the package direction, then pour into a 9 x 9-inch glass pan. Slice the bananas into the Jell-O and refrigerate until firm.

Notes:

Second layer

1 package (3 oz.) lemon Jell-O

1 cup boiling water

4 oz. cream cheese

⅓ cup mayonnaise

Dissolve the Jell-O in the boiling water. Add the cream cheese and mayonnaise; beat mixture until well blended. Refrigerate until partially set; pour over the first layer. Refrigerate until firm.

Third layer

1 package (3 oz.) lime Jell-O

2 cups boiling water

½ cup crushed pineapple

Dissolve Jell-O in the boiling water. When it is cool, add the pineapple. Refrigerate until partially set, and then pour on top of other layers. Refrigerate until firm.

Wilted Dandelion Salad

4 cups dandelion greens, chopped

2 hard-boiled eggs, chopped

2 slices bacon, cooked and crumbled

4 T. flour

1 tsp. salt

3 T. sugar

3 T. vinegar

1½ cups water or milk

Wash the dandelion greens carefully, then drain and chop them and place them in a bowl. Add the hard-boiled eggs.

Fry the bacon in a skillet until crisp. After it has been drained on a paper towel, crumble it and add to bowl of greens. Do not discard the bacon grease.

Combine the rest of the ingredients and add them to the grease in skillet (there should be 2 T. grease; if not, add a small amount of butter or oil). Cook, stirring constantly, until the sauce is smooth and thick. Pour over the dandelion greens and chopped eggs and serve immediately.

Very early in spring, before the flower buds develop, is the time to gather dandelion greens. With a sharp knife, gather the entire plant. Once you are back home, cut off and use only the leaves.

Zesty Oil and Vinegar Dressing

¼ cup vinegar or lemon juice

¾ cup oil

1 tsp. salt

¼ tsp. pepper

½ tsp. paprika

½ tsp. sugar

¼ tsp. dry mustard

1 clove garlic, minced fine (optional)

Combine all ingredients and shake in a jar until well blended. Dressing will separate, but just shake it again when you use it.

Notes:

Quilting bees are a common activity among Amish women, as quilts are used on all beds and given as wedding gifts or made to sell for charity. When the quilt is ready to be put in the frame and quilted, an Amish woman will invite her friends over for the day. She will provide the midday meal, which is often lighter fare than usual, with treats such as homemade grape juice, jam-jams (two sugar cookies stuck together with apple butter or raspberry jam), Tapioca Fluff, and sandwiches. The day will pass quickly as the women expertly stitch, all the while enjoying this special time of visiting and fellowship. They take to heart the saying that "many hands make light work."

VEGETABLES AND SIDE DISHES

The Amish have a preference for farming, taking to heart the admonition found in Genesis 3:23, which states, "The Lord God sent him out of the garden of Eden to till the ground from which he was taken." The weekly farm and produce sales are an opportunity for Amish farmers to sell their products to outside markets, which provides needed cash.

Small farm stands are also commonplace on Amish homesteads—a small building or some tables set up at the end of the lane advertise seasonal produce as well as homemade quilts, jams and jellies, and other goods. Daughters may run these stands, answering questions and making sales. Sometimes, however, the family is busy elsewhere, so a customer might stop to buy garden-fresh produce and find no one in attendance. They pay on the honor system by placing the money owed in a box kept in plain sight for that purpose—even making their own change when necessary.

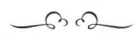

I exhort first of all that supplications, prayers, intercessions, and giving of thanks be made for all men, for kings and all who are in authority, that we may lead a quiet and peaceable life in all godliness and reverence.

1 Timothy 2:2

Lord, I want to be known as a woman who follows You wholeheartedly. I desire Your name to be ever on my lips. And who better to tell Your glorious story to than my own family? May I always be ready to speak of Your saving grace so that their hearts will be ignited with Your holy fire to follow hard after You.

Baked Acorn Squash

Fresh acorn squash (1 squash yields 2 servings)
brown sugar
butter
salt and pepper to taste

Wash squash and cut in half lengthwise (from blossom end to stem end). Scoop out the inside to get rid of seeds and strings. Place cut side up in a lightly greased baking dish or roasting pan. If the squash doesn't stay upright, you can cut off a bit of the bottom rind to make a flat surface. Put a generous amount of brown sugar and butter in each cavity. Season with salt and pepper if desired. Loosely cover with foil and bake at 375° until the squash is soft, at least an hour depending on size.

Baked Acorn Squash with Hamburger Filling

3 acorn squash
1 lb. hamburger
1 cup frozen or fresh corn (sliced off the cob if using fresh)
½ cup tomato sauce
¼ cup celery, finely chopped
¼ cup onion, finely diced
2 T. water
1 T. minced fresh parsley
1 T. prepared mustard
1 tsp. Worcestershire sauce
¼ tsp. allspice
1 tsp. salt
¼ tsp. pepper
bread crumbs

Cut acorn squash in half lengthwise. Spray or brush cut sides with oil and place cut side down on a baking pan that has either been greased or has nonstick aluminum foil placed in the bottom of the pan. Bake at 350° for 30 minutes.

Notes:

The term "Pennsylvania Dutch" is used often when referring to the Amish and other cultural groups that can trace their roots to German-speaking areas in Europe where they spoke a dialect of German referred to as "Deitsch."

Meanwhile, prepare meat filling. Brown the hamburger and drain off the grease. Stir in the corn, tomato sauce, celery, onion, water, parsley, mustard, Worcestershire sauce, allspice, salt, and pepper.

When the squash is almost tender, remove from oven and invert the squash so the cut side is up. Spoon the meat mixture into the cavities and sprinkle with bread crumbs. Return to the oven and bake an additional 30 minutes.

Baked Onions

4 onions, peeled and halved
2 tsp. olive oil or butter
2 tsp. brown sugar
salt and pepper to taste
paprika to taste
1 tsp. lemon juice
minced fresh parsley for garnish

Place the onion halves cut side up in a greased baking pan. Top with the oil or butter, brown sugar, salt, pepper, and paprika and bake at 350° for 1 hour or until onion is tender in the center and deep golden brown. Remove from the oven and drizzle lemon juice over the onions and garnish with parsley before serving.

Baked Sweet Potatoes

4 cups sweet potatoes, cooked, salted, and diced
1 cup brown sugar
1 tsp. flour
½ cup cream
miniature marshmallows

Put the cooked sweet potatoes into a buttered baking pan or casserole dish. Mix together the brown sugar, flour, and cream and pour over the sweet potatoes. Bake at 350° for 20-30 minutes. Remove from oven and cover the top of the sweet potatoes with marshmallows. Return to oven and continue baking until the marshmallows have melted and are golden brown.

Baked Turnips

1½ lb. fresh turnips
¾ tsp. salt
1 T. sugar
⅛ tsp. ground ginger
2 T. fresh parsley, chopped
¼ cup water
3 T. butter

Peel the turnips and cut into ½-inch-thick slices. Place turnips in a buttered baking dish. Combine the salt, sugar, ginger, and parsley and sprinkle over the turnips. Pour the water over the turnips and dot with the butter. Cover tightly and bake at 400° for 50 minutes, stirring occasionally with a fork.

Barley Casserole

1 onion, chopped
6 T. butter
1 cup pearl barley
1 cup hot water
1 can cream of mushroom soup
salt
pepper
garlic
parsley

Sauté onion in butter until softened. Add barley and sauté until golden brown. Turn into a casserole dish, and add water, soup, and seasonings. Mix well. Cover and bake at 350° for at least 1 hour.

Notes:

VEGETABLES AND SIDE DISHES

Notes:

The Amish feel that higher education is not necessary to live a godly life because the goal is to become a good farmer or a good wife, mother, and housekeeper. In 1972 the Supreme Court ruled that Amish children did not need to attend school past the eighth grade. Amish families in a district will build a schoolhouse on private land and all grades will be taught by one or two teachers—often an unmarried woman who also attended school to the eighth grade. However, children are encouraged to study hard and testing has shown that Amish children receive a comparable education to those in public schools.

Broccoli Cheese Casserole

2 T. butter
2 T. flour
¼ tsp. salt
1 3-oz. package cream cheese, softened
¼ cup blue cheese, crumbled
1 cup milk
1 large head broccoli, cooked, drained, and chopped
⅓ cup cracker crumbs, finely crushed (use Ritz crackers)

In a saucepan, melt the butter and then add the flour, salt, and cheeses. Add milk all at once; cook and stir until mixture boils. Stir in chopped broccoli. Turn into a casserole dish and top with cracker crumbs.

Bake at 350° for 30 minutes.

Broccoli with Cheese Sauce

1 head broccoli, cleaned and cut into pieces
4 T. butter
4 T. flour
1 tsp. salt
2 cups milk
¼ lb. mild Cheddar cheese

Cook broccoli in a small amount of water; drain.

While broccoli is cooking, make the cheese sauce. Melt the butter in a medium saucepan and then add the flour and salt, whisking the entire time. Slowly add the milk and continue whisking until the mixture thickens. Add the cheese and continue stirring until the cheese is melted.

In a buttered casserole dish, add half the broccoli and top with half of the cheese sauce. Repeat layers.

Bake at 350° for 20 minutes or until bubbly.

Optional: It's not necessary to oven-bake the casserole; instead, simply serve up helpings of broccoli and spoon the cheese sauce over the top.

Celery and Almonds

3 T. butter
4 cups celery, cut in very thin 3-inch strips
½ cup scallions, finely chopped
1 clove garlic (small), minced
½ cup slivered almonds, toasted

Using a heavy skillet, melt the butter and add the celery. Cook over low heat for about 3 minutes, stirring constantly. Add the scallions and garlic and cook a bit longer, still stirring constantly; do not overcook. To serve, combine the celery mixture with the almonds, reserving a few almonds to sprinkle on top.

Celery and Cheese Casserole

6 cups celery, cut into ½-inch pieces
3 T. butter, divided
¼ cup water
½ tsp. tarragon
2 T. flour
½ cup milk
1 can cream of chicken soup
½ cup Cheddar cheese, shredded
¼ tsp. paprika

Combine celery with 1 T. butter, water, and tarragon in medium saucepan; bring to a boil. Cover. Reduce heat and simmer for 10 minutes. Turn into a 2-quart casserole dish. Set aside.

Heat remaining butter in the same saucepan. Stir in flour. Add milk gradually, stirring constantly until smooth. Add soup; heat thoroughly. Stir in cheese. Pour over celery and mix lightly. Sprinkle with paprika and bake uncovered at 350° for 15 minutes.

Notes:

Notes:

Cheese and Bread Casserole

3 cups soft bread cubes
2 cups Cheddar cheese, shredded
3 eggs
1 tsp. salt
2 cups scalded milk

Layer bread and cheese in a well-buttered casserole dish.

Beat together the eggs, salt, and milk. Pour over the bread and cheese mixture; milk mixture should come to the top of the bread mixture.

Bake at 350° until cooked through and golden brown on top, about 30 minutes.

Company Scalloped Potatoes

6 T. butter
6 T. flour
1 tsp. salt
dash of pepper
1½ cups milk
1½ cups water
2 cups Velveeta cheese, cut into very small cubes
8 cups potatoes, diced and cooked until just tender
3 cups cooked ham, diced
1 cup bread crumbs
4 T. butter, melted

Melt the butter in a saucepan. Remove from heat and add the flour, salt, and pepper, stirring constantly. Continue stirring and gradually stir in milk and water. Return to heat and cook, stirring, until thickened. Add cheese and continue cooking and stirring until cheese is melted. Add potatoes and ham and mix well. Pour potato mixture into a buttered casserole dish. Mix together the bread crumbs and melted butter and put on top of the scalloped potatoes.

Bake uncovered at 350° for 30 minutes or until heated through and scalloped potatoes are golden and bubbly.

Cooked Beets

½ cup sugar

1 tsp. salt

1 T. cornstarch

¼ cup vinegar

¼ cup water

4 cups beets, diced and cooked (you can use canned beets, but see note below)

2 T. butter

In a medium saucepan, mix the sugar, salt, and cornstarch. Add the vinegar and water and stir until smooth. Simmer for about 5 minutes; it will thicken slightly as it cooks. Turn off heat and gently stir in beets. Let stand in saucepan for 30 minutes. Just before serving, bring the beets to a low simmer and add the butter.

If you use canned beats, they are canned with salt and water, so reduce or eliminate the salt. You can also use pickled canned beets. Simply use the beet water to make the sauce and omit the vinegar, sugar, and salt.

Corn Pie

2 cups fresh corn cut from the cob (can use frozen)

1 T. butter, melted and cooled slightly

½ cup milk

2 tsp. salt

1 tsp. sugar

unbaked pie crust, enough for bottom crust and top crust

Mix together the corn, butter, milk, salt, and sugar.

Using a 9-inch pie pan, line the pan with the bottom crust. Fill the pie pan with the corn filling and cover with top crust. Pierce top crust all over with a fork. Bake for 10 minutes in a 400° oven. Reduce heat to 325° and bake an additional 20-25 minutes. Serve hot.

Notes:

The Amish do not believe in making use of government assistance; they pay taxes but do not collect Social Security, nor do they carry health insurance. Instead, when there is a need, such as paying for a lengthy hospital stay, the deacon will oversee administration of funds from a common pool of money, collected from church members to help with the financial burden of the family when necessary.

Notes:

Cottage Cheese-Filled Noodles

2¾ cups flour

2 tsp. salt, divided

1 cup milk

2 eggs, separated

2 cups dry cottage cheese

Sift together the flour and 1 tsp. salt. Add the milk and the egg whites (not the egg yolks; save those for later) and beat well to make a medium soft dough. Roll out fairly thin and cut into 4-inch-square or round pieces.

Mix together the cottage cheese, 1 tsp. salt, and egg yolks. Place some of this filling in the middle of one piece of cut dough and top with another piece of dough. Pinch edges well to seal completely.

Cook in boiling water for 5 minutes. You can serve these with cooked onion, milk gravy, or browned butter.

Creamed Celery and Almonds

4 T. butter, divided

3 cups celery, diced

1 cup slivered almonds

2 T. flour

½ cup half-and-half or cream

⅛ tsp. pepper

1 cup chicken broth, boiling

3 T. Parmesan cheese

Melt 2 T. butter in a large skillet until frothy. Add celery and almonds. Cover and cook for 15 minutes, stirring occasionally. Add 2 more T. butter and let melt. Blend in flour and cook, stirring, for 1 minute. Add half-and-half or cream, pepper, and boiling chicken broth, continuing to stir constantly until sauce comes to a boil and thickens. Spoon casserole into a 1-quart casserole dish and sprinkle with Parmesan cheese. Broil in oven until cheese melts and browns slightly.

Creamed Tomatoes and Onions

4 T. oil
2 large onions, thinly sliced
salt and pepper
4 large tomatoes, skinned and sliced in thirds
¾ cup heavy whipping cream
brown sugar
fresh minced parsley for garnish

Heat the oil in a large skillet, add the sliced onions, cover, and cook over low heat for about 4 minutes. Uncover, stir, and sprinkle with a bit of salt and pepper to taste. Place the tomatoes on top of the onions, cover, and cook for 5 minutes longer; the onions should be tender and golden.

Sprinkle the tomatoes with more salt and pepper and pour the cream over all. Sprinkle the tomatoes with a bit of brown sugar and continue cooking, uncovered, for 3-4 more minutes, or until the cream and tomatoes are heated through. Sprinkle with salt and pepper and serve immediately in bowls, with minced parsley sprinkled on top.

Notes:

Notes:

Garden Supper Casserole

1 cup Cream Sauce (see recipe below)
2 cups soft bread, cubed
½ cup Velveeta or Cheddar cheese, cubed
2 T. butter, melted
1 cup peas
3 hard-boiled eggs, sliced
1 large tomato, sliced

Cream Sauce
3 T. butter
3 T. flour
1 cup milk
¼ tsp. salt

To make cream sauce, melt butter in a saucepan and then add flour; while stirring constantly, slowly pour in milk. Keep stirring and cooking over medium heat until the cream sauce has thickened and comes just to a boil. Season with salt.

Mix together bread, cheese, and melted butter. Spread half of the bread mixture in a buttered casserole dish. Add peas and half the cream sauce. Next, layer on the hard-boiled eggs. Arrange tomato slices over the top and cover with the remainder of the cream sauce. Top that with the remaining bread mixture and bake at 350° for 25 minutes.

Green Beans and Hot Dogs

1 quart jar green beans
5-6 hot dogs, cut up
1 can of cream of mushroom soup

Place green beans in layers in a baking dish with 5-6 cut up hotdogs. Add 1 can of cream of mushroom soup and bake at 350° until the casserole is hot and bubbly.

Green Beans and New Potatoes

½ lb. bacon
2 lb. young green beans, washed and trimmed but left whole
5 new potatoes, unpeeled and cubed
2 small onions, diced
½ tsp. salt
¼ tsp. pepper
1½ cups chicken broth

In a large saucepan, brown the bacon until crisp and pour off grease. Add the beans, potatoes, onions, salt, pepper, and broth; stir. Simmer for 15-20 minutes or until vegetables are tender.

Green Beans with Mustard Sauce

2 lb. small, tender green beans, left whole
¼ cup butter
2 T. prepared mustard
2 T. brown sugar, packed
½ tsp. salt
2 T. lemon juice
3 T. cider vinegar
¼ cup fresh parsley, chopped
¼ tsp. thyme
¼ tsp. pepper

In a large saucepan, cook or steam green beans until tender. Drain and place in a serving dish.

While green beans are cooking, in a small saucepan combine the butter, mustard, brown sugar, salt, lemon juice, vinegar, and seasonings. Heat over low heat until butter has melted and all ingredients are blended. Pour over the hot green beans and serve.

Notes:

The Amish do not like having their pictures taken as they take to heart the admonition in Exodus 20:4, "Thou shalt not make unto thee any graven image, or any likeness of any thing that is in heaven above, or that is in the earth beneath, or that is in the water under the earth" (KJV). They will, however, decorate the walls of their homes with calendar pictures of scenery or animals.

Notes:

Homemade Egg Noodles

6 eggs
4 T. cold water
½ tsp. salt
4 cups flour

Mix together the eggs, water, and salt until well blended. Add flour and knead about 100 times. Roll thin and cut into long strips. Allow to dry thoroughly and store in jars or plastic containers, or use fresh.

Knepp and Asparagus

2 cups flour
¼ tsp. salt
¼ tsp. pepper
4 tsp. baking powder
1 egg, well beaten
3 T. melted butter
enough milk to make a fairly stiff batter
asparagus, cooked and buttered

Sift together the flour, salt, pepper, and baking powder. Stir in the egg, butter, and milk, adding more milk as needed to make a stiff batter.

Bring a pot of water to boiling and, dipping a spoon into the hot water each time, drop spoonfuls of batter into the boiling water. Cook for 15-20 minutes and then drain off the water and put the knepp in a dish that has been greased with butter. Top with cooked, well-buttered asparagus. Salt and pepper to taste and serve immediately.

Onion Fritters

¾ cup flour
1 T. cornmeal
1 T. sugar
2 tsp. baking powder
½ tsp. salt
¼ tsp. pepper
½ cup cold milk
2½ cups onions, finely diced

In a large mixing bowl, whisk together the flour, cornmeal, sugar, baking powder, salt, and pepper. Stir in the milk to make a thick batter, stirring out lumps. Add the onion and mix well again.

Heat oil in a deep-fat fryer or deep-sided frying pan. Drop batter by heaping teaspoonfuls into the hot oil. Fry for a couple of minutes until golden brown on bottom side; turn and fry the other side until golden. Remove with a slotted spoon and serve immediately.

Potluck Potato Casserole

2 lb. potatoes, peeled and diced
½ cup onion, chopped
2 cups Velveeta cheese, cut into small cubes
½ tsp. pepper
1 can cream of chicken soup
½ cup butter, melted
1 pint sour cream
1 tsp. salt
¼ tsp. pepper
2 cups corn flakes, crushed
¼ cup butter, melted

Cook the potatoes until almost soft. Drain. Mix together the onion, Velveeta cheese, pepper, cream of chicken soup, ½ cup butter, sour cream, salt, and pepper. Add to the potatoes and pour mixture into a buttered casserole or baking dish.

Notes:

Mix together the corn flakes and ¼ cup melted butter and cover the potato mixture.

Bake uncovered at 350° for 45 minutes.

Roesti (Browned Potatoes)

¼ cup oil
¾ cup onion, diced
1 26-oz. bag frozen shredded hash browns, unthawed but loose
1 tsp. salt
½ tsp. pepper
¼ cup fresh parsley, minced
1 cup Swiss cheese, shredded

Heat oil in an electric skillet at 275° or use a heavy skillet over medium heat. Add onion and cook until onion is limp and begins to color.

Take the bag of frozen hash browns and give it a good whack on a hard surface to loosen the hash browns; you don't want any clumps of frozen potatoes. Add the potatoes, salt, pepper, and parsley and mix. Take a spatula and press the potato mixture firmly into the bottom of the skillet, making a dense patty.

Increase heat to medium-high, cover, and cook potatoes for 5-8 minutes or until they turn a deep golden brown on the bottom. Don't stir while they are cooking. Turn potatoes, in sections at a time, pat down again firmly, cover, and continue cooking until the bottom is a deep golden brown. Sprinkle the cheese over the top and continue cooking, uncovered, until cheese is melted. Cut into wedges and serve.

Sautéed Onions and Apples

3 T. butter
2 large onions, thinly sliced
6 apples, peeled, cored, and sliced
½ cup brown sugar, packed
1 tsp. cinnamon
salt and pepper to taste

In a large pan or skillet, melt the butter. Add the onions and cook over medium heat for 5 minutes or until onions begin to color. Add the apples on top of the onions; do not stir. Sprinkle on brown sugar, cinnamon, and salt and pepper; again, do not stir.

Cover the pan and cook on low heat, simmering without stirring for 10 minutes. Uncover, turn up heat slightly, and stir lightly to combine the layers. Continue cooking until the apples are completely tender and the juices have been reduced somewhat.

This can be eaten as a vegetable side dish or spooned over pork chops or roast.

Scalloped Carrots

12 carrots, skinned and sliced
4 T. butter
5 T. flour
2 cups milk
½ cup Velveeta cheese, diced
1 small onion, diced
¼ tsp. salt
⅛ tsp. pepper
1 tsp. prepared mustard
crushed potato chips or bread crumbs

Cook carrots in boiling water until tender but not too soft; drain.

Make a white sauce by melting butter in a medium saucepan and adding the flour, stirring constantly. Gradually add the milk, continuing to stir constantly while sauce thickens. Add

Notes:

If you have your own asparagus patch, when harvesting, cut all asparagus tops off below the ground, making sure the cut ends are covered with a bit of loose dirt. This will help the stalk to not "bleed," which takes the strength out of the roots, and next year's crop will be heartier.

VEGETABLES AND SIDE DISHES

Notes:

the cheese and stir until cheese is completely melted. Add the onion, salt, pepper, and mustard and stir carrots into the cheese mixture.

Pour into a buttered casserole dish and top with crushed potato chips or bread crumbs. Bake at 350° for 30-45 minutes or until carrots are thoroughly cooked and casserole is bubbly and golden brown on top.

Scalloped Corn

1 quart canned corn, drained, or 1 quart frozen corn, thawed and drained
1 cup cracker crumbs or bread crumbs
2 eggs, beaten
½ cup milk, approximately
salt and pepper to taste

Place the corn and crumbs in layers in a buttered casserole dish, keeping out a bit of the crumbs to sprinkle on top.

Mix together the eggs, milk, salt, and pepper. Carefully pour over the corn and crumbs; top with a sprinkling of crumbs and bake at 350° for 20 minutes or until bubbly and golden on top.

Velveeta cheese may not seem a likely ingredient found in Amish kitchens, but it's used often because it doesn't need to be refrigerated, is shelf stable, and adds a great taste to many dishes.

Scalloped Rice with Cheese Sauce

¼ cup butter

2 T. onion, diced

2 T. green bell pepper, diced

3 T. flour

½ cup evaporated milk

½ cup water

½ tsp. salt

1 tsp. pepper

1½ cups Cheddar cheese, shredded

½ cup fresh parsley, chopped

3 cups cooked long-grain white rice, divided

4 slices stale bread, processed into crumbs

paprika

In a small saucepan, melt the butter and add onion and green pepper and sauté until the onion begins to color, about 5 minutes. Turn heat to low and add the flour; stirring constantly, until mixture bubbles. Gradually pour in the evaporated milk and water, whisking the entire time until smooth. Add the salt, pepper, cheese, and parsley and continue to whisk until cheese is melted. Stir in 1 cup of the cooked rice.

Put the remaining rice into a well-buttered flat casserole or baking dish and top with the cheese mixture. Sprinkle with the bread crumbs and paprika.

Bake at 375° for 25 minutes or until the top is golden and the casserole is heated through.

Notes:

Notes:

Spinach Pie

3 eggs, beaten
6 potatoes, shredded
1 small onion, diced very fine
4 T. melted butter
1 tsp. salt
pepper to taste
6 cups fresh spinach, chopped very fine

To the eggs add the shredded potatoes and mix well (this will help to keep the raw potatoes from discoloring while making the pie). Add the onion, melted butter, salt, and pepper.

Place half of the potato mixture into the bottom of a buttered baking dish and gently press down. Place the spinach in next and then cover with the remaining potato mixture, pressing down gently again.

Bake at 350° for 30-45 minutes or until done.

The three main sources of energy that the Amish use are waterwheels, windmills, and diesel engines. For those more conservative congregations that do not allow diesel engines to be used for milking machines, the famers sell their milk to cheese plants. Because the milk is boiled during the cheese-making process, they are allowed to milk by hand. But many congregations have allowed the switch because selling grade-A milk is more lucrative than selling milk used in making cheese.

Stewed Tomatoes and Dumplings

Stewed Tomatoes

¼ cup butter
½ cup onion, finely chopped
¼ cup celery, chopped
1 28-ounce can whole tomatoes, coarsely chopped, with juice
2 tsp. brown sugar
½ tsp. salt
½ tsp. dried basil
¼ tsp. pepper

Dumplings

1 cup flour
1½ tsp. baking powder
½ tsp. salt
1 T. butter
1 egg, beaten
6 T. milk
1 T. fresh parsley, minced

In a medium saucepan, melt the butter and sauté the onion and celery about 3 minutes. Add the tomatoes and juice, and the brown sugar and seasonings, and bring to a boil. Simmer uncovered for several minutes.

In a mixing bowl, combine the flour, baking powder, and salt for the dumplings. Cut in the butter using a pastry blender or two knives until the mixture resembles coarse cornmeal. Add the egg, milk, and parsley and blend lightly. Do not overmix. Drop dumplings by tablespoonfuls on top of the simmering tomato mixture. Cover tightly and cook over medium-low heat for 20 minutes. Do not lift the cover during the cooking period. Serve in bowls, topped with butter if desired.

Notes:

You can also use 2 quarts of home-canned stewed tomatoes for this recipe instead of the 28-oz. can. It yields more sauce, which works just fine in this recipe.

VEGETABLES AND SIDE DISHES

Notes:

Summer Squash Casserole

6 cups cubed squash (zucchini, pattypan, crookneck, etc.)
¼ cup onion, chopped
1 can cream of chicken soup
1 cup sour cream
1 cup carrots, shredded
1 8-oz. package herbed stuffing mix
½ cup butter, melted

Cook squash and onion in enough water to cover for 5 minutes; drain.

Mix together the soup, sour cream, and carrots. Gently fold into the squash mixture.

Stir together the stuffing and butter; spoon half of the stuffing in a 12 x 7-inch baking dish. Spread squash mixture over the stuffing and then cover squash with the other half of the stuffing.

Bake at 350° for 30 minutes.

Zucchini and Corn Side Dish

1 T. butter
1 T. oil
6 small zucchini, sliced
3 large ears corn, cooked and cut from cob
1 tsp. sugar
salt and pepper to taste
½ tsp. dill weed (optional)

In a large frying pan or skillet, melt butter and oil until hot, being careful not to let the butter burn. Add the zucchini and fry until golden, 5-6 minutes. Add the corn, sugar, salt, and pepper and cook until corn is heated through. Sprinkle with dill weed if using and serve immediately.

Zucchini Casserole

1½ lb. small zucchini
1 onion, finely chopped
6 T. butter, divided
1 cup Cheddar cheese, shredded
1 tsp. salt
½ tsp. pepper
2 eggs, beaten
1½ cups soft bread crumbs

Scrub zucchini; cook whole in small amount of water until crisp-tender. Cool. Sauté onion in 4 T. butter until golden in color. Cut squash into cubes and add to onion. Stir in cheese, salt, and pepper. Cool slightly. Mix zucchini mixture with the beaten eggs and then spoon into a buttered 1-quart baking dish. Melt remaining 2 T. butter and add to bread crumbs, tossing to coat. Sprinkle crumbs over the top of the zucchini. Bake at 350° for 30-45 minutes or until a knife inserted comes out clean.

Notes:

MAIN DISHES AND CASSEROLES

There is so much to do each day—cleaning the house, weeding the vegetable patch, taking food to an elderly widow or a sister who has recently been ill, or harvesting and canning summer's produce. Casseroles are a good answer for what to feed the family on those busy days. Simply mix together the ingredients and pop the dish into a slow-burning oven to simmer and bake for hours. When the family returns from their day, the aroma from the kitchen beckons them to hurry and sit at their places at the table. The family waits for Father to bow his head and lead the family in silent prayer—then it's time to enjoy what Mother and the girls have prepared.

A typical dinner might consist of Yum-a-Setta, potatoes and carrots from the garden, sliced fresh tomatoes, home-canned applesauce, and cookies and pie for dessert. Water and coffee are often the beverages of choice.

The eyes of all look expectantly to You, and You give them their food in due season. You open Your hand and satisfy the desire of every living thing.
PSALM 145:15-16

Lord, I thank You that I have the means to care for my family. May I always have an open heart and open hands, and when I see others who are struggling, may I be quick to offer help. You have given me so much. Help me to always remember that You desire that I would in turn give to others who are less fortunate.

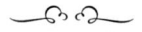

A Husband's Delight

1 lb. hamburger

2 16-oz. cans tomato sauce (or 1 quart home-canned)

1 tsp. salt

1 clove garlic, finely minced

1 T. sugar

1 tsp. pepper

1 T. Worcestershire sauce

1 cup sour cream

1 (3 oz.) package cream cheese

1 onion, finely chopped

1 (8 oz.) package egg noodles, cooked and drained

Brown hamburger in skillet and drain off fat. Add tomato sauce, garlic, Worcestershire, and seasonings and simmer 15 minutes.

Meanwhile, blend together sour cream and cream cheese. Add the onion.

In a buttered baking dish, using half the ingredients, place a layer of noodles. Cover with a layer of meat mixture. Top with cream cheese mixture. Repeat the layers one more time.

Bake at 350° for 30 minutes.

Amish Dressing I

3 eggs

1 cup chicken broth

2 cups milk

1 cup chicken, diced

1 small onion, chopped

¼ cup celery, diced

1½ tsp. salt

1¼ tsp. pepper or to taste

2 quarts dried bread cubes

Beat together eggs, chicken broth, and milk. Add chicken, onion, celery, salt, and pepper and mix well. Add bread cubes and mix well again.

Notes:

There are many variations of Amish Dressing, some of which include chicken, and some that don't. I have included several recipes here that my family has eaten over the years. In actuality, I don't follow an exact recipe (although I have a number of them that I refer to often), but I simply add what I have on hand. You can do the same as you prepare a meal with your family's unique tastes in mind.

Notes:

Place mixture in a buttered rectangular baking dish, cover, and bake at 350° for 1 hour. Take off cover (unless it looks too dry, in which case keep the cover on) and continue baking for 20-30 minutes or until done. If a knife inserted into the middle comes out clean, it's done.

Amish Dressing II

Dressing

6 cups bread crumbs, toasted in the oven until golden
¼ cup celery, diced
1 tsp. dried parsley
1 small onion, diced
2 eggs, beaten
¼ cup butter, melted
salt and pepper to taste

Mix together all the ingredients listed above and add enough hot water to moisten well. Place in a greased casserole dish.

Topping

¼ cup butter
1 T. flour
1 cup chicken broth
2 cans (any combination) of cream of chicken, cream of mushroom, or cream of celery soup

In a medium saucepan, melt the butter, stir in flour; continue stirring while adding broth; keep stirring until mixture thickens. Add the soup and heat through. Pour over the dressing and, taking a fork, poke holes in the dressing so the soup can penetrate.

Bake at 350° for 45 minutes.

Amish Dressing III

4 eggs
½ tsp. salt
⅛ tsp. pepper
½ tsp. sage
½ tsp. thyme
3½-4 cups milk, as needed
1 medium onion, finely chopped
3 stalks celery, finely chopped
¾ cup cooked potatoes, chopped
2 cups cooked chicken, chopped
½ cup cooked carrots, finely diced
1 loaf bread, diced and toasted

Put the eggs into a bowl and beat them. Mix in the salt, pepper, sage, and thyme. Add 2 cups milk, onion, celery, potatoes, chicken, and carrots. Add the bread with enough milk to moisten it well.

Bake in a well-greased casserole dish at 350° for 1½ hours or until the dressing has an omelet-like texture but is not too dry.

Notes:

Notes:

Amish Dressing IV

3 large carrots, diced and cooked
2 large potatoes, diced and cooked
1 cup celery, diced
½ cup onion, diced
½ tsp. sage
1 tsp. salt
½ tsp. pepper
1 cup diced chicken
1 cup chicken broth
1 loaf bread, cubed and toasted
2 T. flour
2 cups milk
1 egg

In a large mixing bowl, mix all the ingredients except the flour, milk, and egg. Put these ingredients in a quart jar with a tight-fitting lid and shake until well blended and frothy. Pour into the bowl with the dressing and toss to mix.

Put the dressing in a well-greased casserole dish and bake at 350° for 1 hour.

Baked Chicken and Apples

1 whole chicken
2 apples, peeled, seeded, and quartered
1 onion, quartered
salt
pepper
1 tsp. parsley
1 tsp. sage
1 tsp. rosemary
1 tsp. thyme
½ tsp. oregano
2 cups hot water
cooked rice

Clean and place the chicken in a deep roaster or casserole dish. Fill the cavity with apples and onion. Sprinkle the salt and pepper and spices around and on top of the chicken. Pour 2 cups hot water into the roasting pan and loosely cover chicken with foil.

Bake at 350° for approximately 1½ hours, or until a meat thermometer inserted into the thickest part of the thigh (but not touching the bone) reads 180°.

The broth will be rich and have a greenish tint. If you think there isn't enough broth for serving, you can add a little more boiling water or broth. To serve, slice the chicken and place on top of the cooked rice on individual plates with deep sides (to hold the broth). Place some of the onion and apple on the side and spoon broth over everything.

Notes:

Notes:

Baked Macaroni and Cheese

2 cups macaroni
2 tsp. salt (for cooking macaroni)
2½ cups milk
8 oz. Velveeta cheese, cubed
salt and pepper to taste
butter
bread crumbs

Cook the macaroni in salted water just until tender; drain. Place the cooked macaroni in a buttered casserole dish. Add the milk, cheese, salt, and pepper. Dot with butter and then top with bread crumbs.

Bake at 350° for 30 minutes or until brown and bubbly.

Beef and Noodle Bake

1 lb. hamburger
¼ cup chopped onion
½ tsp. salt
½ cup diced cheese (Cheddar or Velveeta)
1 egg, beaten
3 cups cooked egg noodles
1 cup tomato juice
2 tsp. Worcestershire sauce
¼ cup catsup
¼ cup cracker or bread crumbs

Brown hamburger and drain off fat. Mix together all the ingredients except crumbs and pour mixture into a greased casserole dish. Top with crumbs and bake at 350° for 1 hour.

Beef and Noodle Casserole

1½ lb. hamburger
1 tsp. salt
½ tsp. pepper
1 T. sugar
2 8-oz. cans tomato sauce
1 cup sour cream
8 oz. cream cheese
½ cup onion, chopped
8-oz. package egg noodles, cooked
½ cup shredded Cheddar cheese

Brown meat; add salt, pepper, sugar, and tomato sauce. Mix together sour cream, cream cheese, and onion. Layer noodles, then cheese mixture, then meat mixture. Repeat, making layers. Cover top with Cheddar cheese.

Bake uncovered for 25-30 minutes at 350°.

Beef and Vegetable Loaf

1½ lb. hamburger
1 egg
1 cup cooked rice
1 small onion, chopped
1 carrot, minced
5 T. fresh parsley, chopped and divided
1 tsp. salt
⅛ tsp. pepper
½ cup milk

Mix hamburger with egg, rice, onion, carrot, 4 T. of parsley, salt, pepper, and milk until well blended.

Pat into a bowl-shaped loaf and place in a greased, shallow baking pan. Sprinkle top with remaining parsley.

Bake at 350° for 1 hour.

Notes:

Notes:

Braised Beef Cubes

2 lb. stew meat, cubed
2 T. oil
1 small onion, chopped
2 cans cream of mushroom soup
1 package onion soup mix, dry
1 can water
salt and pepper to taste
1 cup sour cream
cooked rice

Brown the stew meat in the oil. Add onion and continue to cook for several minutes until onion is limp. Add the soup, dry soup mix, water, salt, and pepper. Cover and simmer on low for about 45 minutes or until meat is tender. When ready to serve, add the sour cream and heat thoroughly but do not boil.

Serve on a bed of rice.

Busy Day Ham Casserole

1½ cups cooked ham, cubed
1 cup potatoes, diced
1 cup carrots, diced
½ cup peas, fresh or frozen
½ cup canned green beans
1 T. flour
your favorite biscuit recipe
½ cup grated Cheddar cheese
1 tsp. dried parsley
salt and pepper to taste

Brown the ham in a small amount of oil and then add the potatoes, carrots, and enough water so they don't stick while cooking. Cook until tender and then add the peas, green beans, and just enough boiling water to cover them.

Stir together the flour with enough cold water to make a very thin paste. Add this to the meat and vegetables while stirring constantly. Pour mixture into a large casserole or baking dish with sides that give plenty of room for mixture to bubble up while baking.

Drop biscuit dough, to which you add the cheese, parsley, and salt and pepper, on top of the casserole and bake at 350° for 20-30 minutes or until done.

Cabbage Casserole with Hamburger

2 heads cabbage, chopped
1 lb. hamburger
½ cup onion, chopped
1 pint sour cream
1 large can tomato juice (about 1 quart)
1 cup Cheddar cheese, shredded

Boil the cabbage and drain. Brown the hamburger and onion; drain.

In a large bowl, mix everything together, pour into a large baking dish, and bake at 400° for 45 minutes. (Check the casserole while baking and turn down the oven temperature if it looks as though your casserole is browning too quickly.)

Notes:

In recent years, some Amish families have earned money by preparing and serving meals to groups of tourists. These groups are served many of the recipes found in this book...nothing gourmet, but rib-sticking meals that the Amish eat every day. They finish these hearty meals off with a variety of pies, and no one goes away hungry.

Notes:

It might come as a surprise to learn that the Amish are not adverse to credit cards. But it depends on the area—some congregations use credit cards regularly, while others do not.

Calico Beans

1 lb. hamburger
5 strips bacon, chopped
1 large onion, chopped
½ cup catsup
¾ cup brown sugar
1 T. prepared mustard
1 T. vinegar
1 15-oz. can baked beans
1 15-oz. can kidney beans
1 1-oz. can butter beans

In a skillet, brown the hamburger, bacon, and onion. Drain.

In a large bowl, mix together the catsup, brown sugar, mustard, and vinegar. Drain the beans and mix them together with the above ingredients. Add the hamburger mixture and mix well again.

Put into a baking pan and bake at 325° for 1 hour.

Chicken and Pimento Loaf

1 cup bread crumbs
½ cup milk
3 cups cooked chicken, diced
1 tsp. salt
½ tsp. pepper
3 eggs, separated
2 T. melted butter
¼ cup chopped pimentos

In a large bowl, mix together the bread crumbs and milk and let stand 10 minutes to soften crumbs. Then add the chicken, salt, pepper, egg yolks, butter, and pimentos and mix well.

Beat the egg whites until stiff and fold them into the chicken mixture. Butter a large loaf pan or square baking dish and spoon the chicken mixture into the prepared pan.

Bake at 350° for 45 minutes.

Chicken Party Buns

1 package cream cheese, softened
1 cup cooked chicken (you can also use leftover turkey)
1 tsp. lemon juice
½ cup mayonnaise
2 T. diced celery
2 T. diced onion
2 T. diced green pepper
2 chopped hard-boiled eggs
1 package hamburger buns

Mix together all the ingredients except for the buns. Pile the chicken mixture onto the hamburger buns and wrap each of them in aluminum foil.

Bake at 400° for 10 minutes, then reduce heat to 325° and continue baking for an additional 30 minutes.

Chicken Potpie

5 lb. meaty chicken pieces on the bone
2 carrots, halved
3 stalks celery, halved
1 onion, quartered
1 bay leaf
salt and pepper to season
Potpie Sauce (recipe follows)
pastry for a double crust, unbaked

In a large stockpot, combine the chicken, carrots, celery, onion, bay leaf, salt, and pepper. Cover completely with water. Cover the pot and bring contents to a boil. Reduce heat and simmer for 30 minutes or until chicken is done and vegetables are tender; do not drain broth. Remove the chicken from the pot and cool slightly so you can remove the meat from the bones. Remove the carrots, chop them, and set aside.

Strain the broth through a sieve into a large bowl and discard the remainder of the vegetables. Allow the broth to cool so the

Potpies usually have a top crust only. Because this recipe makes a large batch, making enough pastry for a double crust will ensure that there will be enough crust to completely cover the top of the potpie.

Notes:

fat will separate; skim off fat and discard. Measure out 5 cups of the strained broth to use for the sauce.

Potpie Sauce

⅓ cup butter
½ cup flour
5 cups chicken broth
1 tsp. thyme
¾ tsp. salt
¼ tsp. powdered mustard
½ tsp. pepper
½ cup peas, fresh or frozen, thawed
½ cup chopped fresh parsley

In a large saucepan, melt the butter over medium heat. Add the flour and stir constantly until mixture bubbles in pan. Add the chicken broth and whisk constantly until mixture bubbles and thickens. You may need to add a bit more broth if mixture becomes too thick. Stir in the seasonings and then add the chicken, carrots, peas, and parsley. Mix well.

Transfer the chicken and sauce mixture to a greased 13 x 9-inch glass baking dish. Roll out pastry thick (to fit the top of the dish) and place it over the chicken filling. Crimp edges just as you would a pie; slash crust in several places to vent the steam while baking.

Bake at 350° for 1 hour. Cool for 10 minutes on a wire rack before serving.

Many Amish families raise hogs for meat and, being frugal, they use just about everything; the saying goes that the only part of the hog that is wasted is the squeal.

Chicken Tetrazzini

1 4-lb. chicken
4 cups broth (reserved from cooking chicken)
8-9 T. flour
1 can cream of mushroom soup
2 cups egg noodles, cooked and drained
½ lb. Velveeta cheese, cubed
2 T. butter
4 cups bread crumbs
½ cup cream or milk

Stew chicken in water to cover until meat is thoroughly cooked and tender. Reserve 4 cups broth. Cool chicken enough to handle; skin and debone and cut meat into bite-sized pieces.

Take a small portion of the broth and mix with the flour to make a thin paste. In a large pot, heat the rest of the broth, and when it boils add the flour paste, stirring constantly until it thickens. Remove from heat and add soup. Mix well. Add the cooked noodles, cheese, and chicken. Season with salt and pepper to taste. Put in a buttered 9 x 13-inch baking dish.

In a saucepan, melt the butter; add the bread crumbs and brown slightly. Add the cream or milk to the crumb mixture and mix. Put bread crumbs over the top of the chicken and noodles and bake at 325° for 30 minutes.

Notes:

MAIN DISHES AND CASSEROLES

Notes:

Creamy Chicken Bake

½ cup flour
¾ tsp. salt
½ tsp. pepper
½ tsp. paprika
1½ tsp. poultry seasoning
2 T. butter
2 T. oil
8 pieces chicken
2 cups heavy cream

In a large bag, combine the flour, salt, pepper, paprika, and poultry seasoning. In a large saucepan or frying pan, melt together the butter and oil. Shake the chicken pieces in the flour mixture and then brown them on both sides in the butter and oil.

Transfer the chicken pieces to a large baking dish and pour the cream over the chicken. Sprinkle with additional paprika, cover, and bake at 300° for 2 hours. When serving, ladle the pan gravy over the chicken.

Creamy Noodle and Hamburger Casserole

2 cups sour cream

2 cups small-curd cottage cheese

¼ cup onion, chopped

2 T. fresh parsley, minced

1 8-oz. package egg noodles

1 T. oil

2 lb. hamburger

2 6-oz. cans tomato paste

1 T. basil

1 T. oregano

1 tsp. salt

½ tsp. pepper

In a small mixing bowl, combine the sour cream, cottage cheese, onion, and parsley; set aside.

Cook the noodles per directions on package; drain and set aside.

Heat oil in a large skillet and brown hamburger; drain off grease. Add tomato paste, basil, oregano, salt, and pepper and simmer for 5 minutes.

Grease a rectangular baking dish and layer as follows: meat sauce, noodles, and sour cream mixture. Repeat layers and end with the meat sauce. Bake at 325° for 1 hour. Let stand for 5 or 10 minutes before serving.

Notes:

Notes:

Enchilada Casserole

1 lb. hamburger
¼ cup onion, chopped
1 can diced tomatoes with peppers (spicy), undrained
1 can tomato sauce
1 package taco seasoning
1 can cream of mushroom soup
1 large package corn tortillas
1 cup Cheddar cheese, shredded
sliced black olives

In large saucepan, brown the hamburger and onion; drain off fat. Add the tomatoes, tomato sauce, taco seasoning, and cream of mushroom soup. Mix well and heat to just boiling. Tear the tortillas into large bite-sized pieces and put them in the meat sauce, pushing them down into the sauce. Keep adding pieces of tortilla until you can no longer push any more into the sauce. Reduce heat to low, cover, and let simmer for about 5 minutes. Serve with cheese and olives.

Fidget Pie

1 lb. potatoes, peeled and thinly sliced
salt and pepper to taste
½ tsp. dried sage
½ tsp. ground nutmeg
3 cups cooked ham, diced
1 medium onion, thinly sliced
1 lb. cooking apples, peeled, cored, and sliced
1¼ cups chicken broth
pastry for single crust pie

Preheat oven to 425°. Butter a deep dish pie plate or round casserole dish.

Layer potato slices in the bottom of the dish. Season with salt, pepper, sage, and nutmeg. Continue layering and seasoning in this order: ham, then onion, and finally apples. Pour broth over all.

Roll out pastry. Fit pastry over pie, and seal and flute edge. Take a knife and cut a cross in the middle of the pastry to vent steam while the pie is baking.

Bake at 425° for 15 minutes. Reduce heat to 350° and continue to bake for another 40-45 minutes.

Filsa

2 cups milk

4 eggs

½ cup celery, chopped

½ cup carrots, chopped

½ cup potatoes, cubed (small)

1 cup cooked chicken meat, chopped, with broth

½ tsp. pepper

½ tsp. sage

½ tsp. thyme

1 tsp. salt

2 cups toasted bread crumbs

In a small bowl, mix together the milk and eggs. In a large bowl, combine all the other ingredients and then add the milk and egg mixture and stir to blend. Put in a baking pan and bake at 350° for 45 minutes or until golden brown. Good served with milk or chicken gravy.

Notes:

German Meatballs and Sauerkraut

1 lb. hamburger
½ lb. ground pork
¾ cup bread crumbs
½ cup onion, finely diced
1 T. fresh parsley, chopped
1½ tsp. salt
⅛ tsp. pepper
1 tsp. Worcestershire sauce
1 egg, beaten
½ cup milk
2-3 T. oil for frying
1 27-oz. can sauerkraut, undrained (or use homemade)

In a mixing bowl, combine the meats, bread crumbs, onion, parsley, salt, pepper, Worcestershire sauce, egg, and milk and mix well. Shape into 2-inch balls.

Heat the oil in a skillet and brown the meatballs. Remove and drain the fat from the skillet. Spoon the sauerkraut into the skillet and top with the meatballs. Cover and simmer 15-20 minutes or until meat is completely cooked. Add water if necessary during cooking so the dish doesn't become too dry.

German Rye Meatballs

2 cups soft rye bread crumbs

1 16-oz. can sauerkraut, drained

2 eggs, lightly beaten

½ cup milk

½ cup onion, chopped

1 tsp. caraway seeds

½ tsp. pepper

2 T. catsup

2 lb. hamburger (use lean meat)

In a large bowl, combine all ingredients except meat and mix well. Add the hamburger and mix thoroughly.

Pack into a loaf approximately 10 x 8 inches and place on a rack in a foil-lined 9 x 13-inch baking pan.

Bake for 1¼ hours, or until nicely browned. Let stand for several minutes before slicing.

Notes:

There are three main types of buggies used by the Amish: the market wagon, family buggy, and the courting buggy, and they are made and repaired by their own carriage makers. All buggies are required by law to have lights and turn signals, and these are battery operated. In addition, each buggy has a slow-moving triangle symbol on the rear and flashing lights for nighttime driving.

Notes:

Ham Loaf

Ham Loaf

½ cup minute tapioca
¾ cup milk
1 cup bread crumbs
2 lb. ground ham or 1 lb. each ground ham and lean pork
2 eggs, beaten
½ cup onion, chopped fine
salt and pepper to taste

Glaze Topping

¼ cup vinegar
¼ cup water
½ cup brown sugar
1 T. prepared mustard

Mix tapioca and milk. Add bread crumbs and let stand for 10 minutes.

Meanwhile, combine the ingredients for the glaze in a small saucepan and heat gently until brown sugar is melted. Set aside.

Combine ham, eggs, onion, salt, and pepper. Add milk mixture and mix thoroughly. Pat into a loaf pan or shape into a loaf and place in a baking dish. Pour glaze over the top and bake at 325° for 1½ hours or until done.

Hamburger Gravy and Mashed Potatoes

1 lb. hamburger
4 T. oil or butter
5-6 T. flour
1 quart hot water
Kitchen Bouquet liquid seasoning
salt and pepper to taste
mashed potatoes

In a heavy pot, brown hamburger; do not drain off fat. Add oil or butter (or a combination of the two) and melt butter over medium heat, stirring occasionally. Stir in 5-6 T. flour, depending on how lean or fat the hamburger was and therefore how much grease there is to work with. Stirring constantly, slowly add the water and continue stirring until thickened. Add Kitchen Bouquet and salt and pepper.

Serve over mashed potatoes.

Hamburger Macaroni

1 lb. hamburger
1 cup onion, chopped
1 cup celery, diced
1 clove garlic, minced
½ cup green bell pepper, diced
2 cups uncooked elbow macaroni
2 8-oz. cans tomato sauce
1¼ cups water
¼ cup fresh snipped parsley or 4 T. dried
1 tsp. salt
½ tsp. pepper
2 T. Worcestershire sauce
1 cup Cheddar cheese, shredded

Brown hamburger and pour off most of fat. Remove meat from the skillet and set aside. In the remaining fat, sauté the onion,

Notes:

The Amish meet on alternate Sundays in a church member's home. The service lasts about four hours, and a light dinner is served afterward before everyone goes home for evening chores. The young people will often go to another home for a light supper and then go to another farm for an evening hymn singing that will often last until midnight.

Notes:

celery, garlic, and green pepper until crisp-tender. Remove vegetables from the skillet and set aside.

Add 1 T. oil to the skillet and brown macaroni just until lightly golden. Return meat and vegetables to the skillet. Add remainder of ingredients except for cheese. Simmer, covered, for 25 minutes or until macaroni is done. Top with cheese and serve.

Hamburger Pie with Onion Biscuits

Filling
1½ lb. hamburger
1 medium onion, chopped
1 can tomato soup
salt and pepper to taste

In a medium saucepan, cook the hamburger and onion until well browned. Drain off grease. Add the soup, salt, and pepper and heat thoroughly. Pour into a greased casserole pan.

Onion Biscuits
1½ cup sifted flour
1½ tsp. baking powder
½ tsp. salt
1 tsp. celery seed
¼ cup shortening
½ cup onion, chopped fine
1 egg, beaten
⅓ cup milk

Mix together the flour, baking powder, salt, and celery seed. Cut in the shortening until mixture resembles small peas. Add the onion.

Combine the egg and milk and add to the flour mixture. Mix until it forms a ball. Turn out onto a lightly floured surface and knead about 10 times. Roll out and, using a biscuit cutter, cut out the biscuits and place them on top of the meat mixture.

Place in a preheated 425° oven. After about 5 minutes, reduce heat to 375° and bake for another 20 minutes or until biscuits are done.

Hamburger Roll-Ups with Gravy

Filling

1 lb. hamburger
1 onion, chopped
1 T. oil
½ tsp. salt
pinch of pepper
2 T. flour
½ cup milk
biscuit dough

Gravy

1 can cream of mushroom soup
½ cup milk
½ cup chili sauce

Brown the hamburger and onion in the oil; drain off some of the grease. Season with salt and pepper. Add the flour, stirring, and then gradually add the milk, continuing to stir until meat mixture thickens. Remove from heat and allow to cool so it doesn't burn when you handle the roll-ups.

Roll out the biscuit dough in a wide rectangle to about a ½-inch thick. Spread the meat filling over the dough. Roll up into a log the way you do when making cinnamon rolls. Cut the log into 1½-inch slices. Place the roll-ups cut side up on an ungreased pan and bake at 375° for 20-30 minutes or until done.

In the meantime, simmer together the gravy ingredients and spoon over the baked roll-ups when ready to serve, or plate the roll-ups and pass the gravy in a bowl.

Notes:

Haystack Supper

40 saltine crackers, crushed
2 cups cooked rice
3 lb. hamburger
1 large onion, chopped
1½ cups tomato juice
¾ cup water
3 T. taco seasoning
salt and pepper to taste
4 cups lettuce, shredded
3 medium tomatoes, diced
½ cup butter, cubed
½ cup flour
4 cups milk
1 lb. Velveeta cheese, cubed
3 cups sharp Cheddar cheese, shredded
1 can pitted olives
1 package tortilla chips (14½ oz.)

This recipe makes enough for 2 casseroles, so you will be dividing the ingredients into 2 baking dishes.

Divide crackers between two ungreased 13 x 9-inch baking dishes. Top each with rice.

In a large skillet, brown the hamburger and onion; drain. Add the tomato juice, water, and seasonings and simmer for 20 minutes. Spoon meat mixture over rice. Next, layer on the lettuce and tomatoes.

In a large saucepan, melt the butter. Stir in the flour and continue stirring until smooth. Gradually add the milk. Continue stirring, bring to a boil, and cook until the sauce thickens, about 2 minutes. Reduce heat to low and stir in Velveeta cheese until melted. Pour cheese mixture over the lettuce and tomatoes.

Top with Cheddar cheese and olives and serve with the tortilla chips.

Hobo Dinner

1 lb. hamburger
¼ cup milk
salt and pepper to taste
6 large potatoes, peeled and sliced
2 onions, sliced
¼ lb. Velveeta cheese, cubed
1 can cream of mushroom soup

Press hamburger into the bottom of a 2½ quart casserole dish. Pour milk over the meat. Sprinkle on some salt and pepper. Next, layer on the potatoes, then the onions, and then the cheese. Mix about a quarter of a can of water with the soup and pour it over everything.

Bake at 350° for 1 hour or until potatoes are tender.

Hot Sauce Beef and Rice

1½ lb. round steak, cubed
2 T. butter
½ onion, diced
1½ tsp. salt
¼ tsp. chili powder
1 clove garlic, minced
¼ tsp. cinnamon
½ cup celery, chopped
2 T. prepared mustard
1 cup water
cooked rice

Brown steak in butter. Stir in all remaining ingredients except rice and simmer, covered, for 1-1½ hours or until meat is tender. Add water if necessary. Serve over cooked rice.

Notes:

The Amish rarely speak English in the home, and young children usually learn English when they begin attending school. In the home, a German or Swiss dialect is spoken, but high German is used at church services, which is also taught at school. As a result, Amish children will not understand much of the service until they reach the fourth or fifth grade, but the Amish believe first comes discipline and then comes understanding.

Notes:

Individual Beef Potpies

1 beef bouillon cube

2 cups boiling water

3½ cups cooked beef, chopped, or cooked hamburger

2 tsp. Worcestershire sauce

1½ tsp. salt

1 tsp. sugar

½ tsp. paprika

¼ tsp. pepper

1 package (10 oz.) frozen mixed vegetables

¼ cup flour

pastry (see below)

Dissolve the bouillon cube in the boiling water and add the beef, Worcestershire sauce, salt, sugar, paprika, and pepper. Add the vegetables and cook the mixture for 5 minutes. Combine the flour with enough cold water to make a thin paste and slowly stir it into the meat and vegetables. Continue stirring and cooking until mixture thickens. Keep warm. When you have made the pastry, spoon the meat and vegetable mixture into 6 individual oven-proof custard cups or ramekins that are about 6-8 ounces each. Do not overfill.

Pastry

1 cup flour

½ cup cornmeal

¾ tsp. salt

⅓ cup shortening

4 T. cold water

Sift together the flour, cornmeal, and salt. Cut in the shortening until the mixture resembles coarse crumbs. Sprinkle the water by tablespoonfuls over the mixture and stir it lightly with a fork until just damp. Then, using your hands, work dough gently and as little as possible until the dough holds together and forms a ball. You might need to add a bit more cold water.

Divide dough into 6 parts and roll each to form a circle large enough to fit over the top of the meat and vegetable mixture in each baking cup. Turn under and crimp edges. Make several cuts in the pastry to allow steam to escape while baking.

Bake at 450° for 12-15 minutes.

Konigsberger Klopse

1½ lb. hamburger
2 slices bread, soaked quickly in water and then squeezed dry
3 eggs
1 onion, chopped
salt and pepper to taste
6 cups boiled potatoes, cut into chunks
Sour Cream Sauce (see below)

Mix together the hamburger, bread, eggs, onion, salt, and pepper. Form into balls the size of walnuts and drop them into a pot of boiling salted water. (Use about 1½ quarts of water for cooking.) Cook the balls for 10 minutes and then place them in a roasting pan or casserole dish with the potatoes, reserving 1 cup of the water used to cook meatballs.

Sour Cream Sauce

1 cup strained cooking water from meatballs
1 cup sour cream
1 cup milk
4 T. flour
salt and pepper to taste
capers (optional)

In a large jar with a tight-fitting lid, shake together all the ingredients for the Sour Cream Sauce, except for the capers, making sure there are no flour lumps. Heat mixture over low heat in a medium saucepan, and when hot pour over the meatballs in the roasting pan.

Bake at 350° for 45 minutes. Sprinkle with capers and serve.

Notes:

Notes:

Lasagna Casserole

1 lb. hamburger
2 cloves garlic or 1 tsp. garlic powder
2 T. oil
1 8-oz. can tomato sauce
1 #2 can tomatoes (2½ cups)
1½ tsp. salt
¼ tsp. oregano
8 oz. lasagna noodles, cooked
½ lb. mozzarella cheese
¾ lb. cottage cheese
½ cup Parmesan cheese

Sauté hamburger and garlic in oil. Add tomato sauce, tomatoes, salt, and oregano. Simmer for 20 minutes. Cook noodles; drain.

In a greased lasagna pan, alternate layers of noodles, mozzarella cheese, cottage cheese, meat sauce, and parmesan cheese, ending with meat sauce and parmesan cheese.

Bake at 375° for 1 hour.

Leftover Turkey Croquettes

leftover turkey
leftover dressing
gravy or broth
flour
egg, beaten
bread or cracker crumbs
oil for frying

Cut up turkey into very small bits. Mix 2 parts turkey to 1 part dressing. Add a bit of gravy or broth to moisten. Form into patties and freeze until needed.

To use, thaw the patties and then dredge them first in flour, then in beaten egg, and then in bread or cracker crumbs. Fry in oil until golden brown on each side.

Liver and Vegetable Skillet

4 strips bacon
1 lb. liver
3 T. flour
¼ tsp. salt
¼ tsp. pepper
1 cup carrots, sliced
1 cup celery, sliced
2 cups onions, sliced
2 potatoes, pared and quartered
1 cup tomato juice

In a large skillet, fry bacon until crisp and remove from pan; do not discard grease.

Coat liver with a mixture of the flour, salt, and pepper; brown liver in the bacon grease.

Arrange the vegetables over the liver and sprinkle with a bit more salt; pour tomato juice over the top and cover.

Simmer for 30-40 minutes. Sprinkle with crumbled bacon when ready to serve.

Meatballs and Gravy

1 lb. hamburger
½ cup carrots, shredded
½ cup potatoes, shredded
¼ cup onion, finely chopped
salt and pepper to taste
1 can cream of celery soup (or another favorite cream soup)
1 can water

Mix together all ingredients except soup and water; roll into 1-inch balls. Brown in a skillet and then place meatballs in a casserole dish.

Combine the soup and water and mix well. Pour soup over meatballs and bake at 350° for 45-60 minutes.

Notes:

Many Amish families rent locker space to store their frozen foods, but they also have an ice box at home for storing small amounts of food. The ice man still drops by Amish farms today to sell blocks of ice that are used in these old-fashioned boxes, but this wasn't always so. In earlier times, for those Amish housewives who were not fortunate to live in an area that could sustain an ice house for the summer, they would resort to other methods to preserve their food. Canning, drying or dehydrating, "painting" whole bolognas with wax, burying pork ribs in fat, and putting eggs for baking in lime water are just some of the resourceful ways these women managed.

Notes:

Meatballs and Mushroom Gravy

4 lb. hamburger
1 cup celery, finely diced
1 medium onion, finely diced
4 eggs
3 tsp. salt
1 tsp. pepper
1 can cream of mushroom soup
1 can milk

Combine all ingredients except for the soup and milk. Mix well and shape into balls. Brown the meatballs in butter or oil and arrange them in a roaster.

In a small saucepan, mix together the cream of mushroom soup and milk and heat. Pour over meatballs and bake at 350° for 45 minutes.

Meat Loaf and Mashed Potatoes

2 lb. lean hamburger
1 cup cracker crumbs
1 medium onion, diced
3 eggs
½ cup catsup
1 tsp. salt
½ tsp. pepper
mashed potatoes
½ cup Velveeta cheese, cut in thin slices

Mix together the hamburger, cracker crumbs, onion, eggs, catsup, salt, and pepper. Shape into a loaf. Place in a baking dish and bake at 350° for 1 hour or until done. (There should be no pink to the meat.) Top with mashed potatoes and Velveeta cheese and return to the oven for another 15 minutes.

Meat Loaf and Potatoes

2 cups potatoes, thinly sliced
¼ cup plus 1 T. onion, chopped
2 tsp. salt, divided
pepper to taste
1 lb. hamburger
¾ cup milk
½ cup saltine crackers, crushed
¼ cup catsup

Combine potatoes, 1 T. onion, salt, and pepper in a greased casserole dish. Mix together the hamburger, milk, crackers, catsup, ¼ cup onion, salt, and pepper and spread over the top of the potatoes.

Bake at 350° for 1 hour or until the potatoes are tender and the meat is thoroughly cooked.

Muffin Burgers

1½ lb. hamburger, lean
1½ cups fresh bread crumbs
1 tsp. dehydrated minced onion
½ tsp. dry mustard
1 cup applesauce

Combine the meat, bread crumbs, onion, and mustard. Add the applesauce and mix thoroughly. Let stand until the applesauce has moistened the ingredients.

Divide into 12 equal parts and pack into ungreased muffin tins.

Bake at 350° for 30 minutes.

Notes:

A little baking powder added to meat loaf will make it lighter and give a better taste. A teaspoon of baking powder added to each quart of potatoes while mashing will make them fluffy, smooth, and more tasty.

Notes:

Old-Fashioned Beef Hash

3 cups leftover roast beef
1 medium onion, diced
1 cup mashed potatoes
1½ tsp. salt
1½ cups milk
½ cup bread crumbs

Chop the meat and onion very fine. Add the mashed potatoes, salt, and milk and mix well. Place in a buttered casserole dish and top with the bread crumbs.

Bake at 350° for 30 minutes.

Oven-Baked Chicken I

1 egg
1 cup milk
1 cup cornflakes, crushed
1 cup soda crackers, crushed
2 tsp. salt
2 T. seasoned salt
1 tsp. pepper
2 young broilers or fryers, cut up

In a medium bowl, mix together the egg and milk and whisk until well blended.

In another bowl, mix together the cornflakes, soda crackers, salt, seasoned salt, and pepper.

Dip the chicken pieces into egg and milk mixture, roll in the crumbs, and place on a buttered cookie sheet or jelly roll pan.

Bake at 375° for 30 minutes. Turn meat, reduce heat to 350°, and bake for another 30-45 minutes or until chicken is thoroughly cooked.

Oven-Baked Chicken II

½ cup flour
2 tsp. paprika
1 tsp. pepper
¼ tsp. dry mustard
3 tsp. salt
1 young broiler or young chicken, cut into pieces
1 stick butter, melted

Mix together the dry ingredients in a plastic bag. Drop chicken pieces into the bag and shake well.

Place the melted butter in a large baking pan or roaster. Add the chicken, being careful not to crowd the pieces.

Bake at 350° for 1-2 hours or until done, turning chicken halfway through baking.

Oven-Baked Chicken III

⅓ cup oil
⅓ cup butter, melted
½ cup flour
½ cup cracker meal
½ cup cornmeal
1½ tsp. garlic salt
1½ tsp. paprika
1½ tsp. sage
1 tsp. salt
1 tsp. pepper
¼ tsp. red pepper flakes
4 lbs. chicken pieces

Combine the oil and butter in a shallow baking pan, such as a jelly roll pan.

In a large paper or plastic sack, combine the flour, cracker meal, cornmeal, and seasonings.

Roll the chicken pieces in the melted oil and butter mixture and

Notes:

Most of the clothing the Amish wear is homemade, although men's good wool suits are often purchased from an Amish tailor. A bolt of fabric will be purchased and everyone in the family will get a new dress or shirt from the same fabric. Amish women do not have an extensive wardrobe, and the style rarely changes. All they really need is "one for wash, one for wear, one for dress, and one for spare." And because the style is timeless, hand-me-downs are in great demand. All the clothing and household goods that a woman produces are made on a treadle sewing machine—they can buy a "modern" sewing machine, but it must be refitted with a treadle apparatus.

Notes:

place them in the bag, three at a time. Shake to coat the chicken. Remove the chicken pieces and place them on waxed paper. Repeat until all chicken pieces have been coated.

Place the coated chicken pieces on the jelly roll pan that has the butter and oil, skin side down. Bake at 375° for 45 minutes. Using a spatula, turn the pieces and bake an additional 10 minutes or until both sides are golden.

Overnight Ham and Macaroni Casserole

1 cup uncooked macaroni
1 can cream of mushroom soup
3 T. butter, melted
½ cup onion, diced
1 cup cooked ham, diced
1½ cup milk
1 cup Velveeta cheese, diced

Mix together all the ingredients and refrigerate at least 8 hours or overnight. Stir several times.

Bake at 350° for 1½-2 hours

Oyster Filling

4 cups dry bread cubes
½ cup butter
1 small onion, diced fine
1 stalk celery, chopped fine
1 pint oysters, shucked and chopped fine, reserving liquid
1 cup milk
salt and pepper to taste

If using fresh bread, cube the bread the day before and put in a large baking pan, cover with a towel, and let set so the bread cubes dry out somewhat.

The next day, melt the butter in a saucepan, add the onion and celery, and sauté on medium-low heat for 5 minutes. Add the oysters along with their liquid and continue to cook for another 2 minutes. Turn off heat and add the milk, and then add salt and pepper to taste.

Put the bread cubes in a large mixing bowl and add the oyster mixture. Mix well, making sure that the bread crumbs are moist but not too wet. Add a bit more milk or bread, if needed.

Place the prepared filling in a buttered casserole dish (a rectangular one works well) and bake at 350° for 1 hour.

Penny Supper

6 hot dogs, sliced into "pennies"
4 cooked potatoes, diced
3 T. onion, chopped
¼ cup butter, melted
1 tsp. mustard
1 can cream of mushroom soup
salt and pepper to taste

Combine the hot dogs, potatoes, onion, and butter. Place in a baking dish.

Mix together the remaining ingredients and gently fold into the hot dog mixture. Cover with aluminum foil and bake at 350° for 25 minutes.

Notes:

When this country was a lot younger and settlements were sometimes miles apart, the Amish had a long way to travel by horse and buggy for church. So after services, a light lunch was served before the long drive home. Not much has changed over the years, and the tradition is still going strong today.

Notes:

Pizza Casserole

¼ cup onion, diced
¼ cup bell pepper, diced
½ stick butter
8 oz. thin spaghetti noodles, cooked and drained
2 16-oz. jars pizza sauce
4 oz. pepperoni, sliced thin
8 oz. sausage, browned and drained
4 oz. Swiss cheese, shredded and divided
4 oz. mushrooms, sliced (or a small can of mushrooms, drained)
¼ tsp. salt
¼ tsp. pepper
½ tsp. oregano

Sauté onion and pepper in butter. Drain the butter into the bottom of a 9 x 13-inch baking dish. Cover with spaghetti. Spread 1 jar of pizza sauce over spaghetti. Layer pepperoni, sausage, half of the cheese, onions, peppers, mushrooms, and spices on top. Cover with the second jar of pizza sauce and the remainder of the cheese.

Cover the casserole dish with aluminum foil, making sure the foil doesn't touch the cheese. Bake at 350° for 45 minutes.

Poor Man's Steak

1 lb. hamburger
1 cup milk
1 cup cracker crumbs
¼ tsp. pepper
1 tsp. salt
1 small onion, chopped
1 can cream of mushroom soup
½ can water

Combine all ingredients except the soup and water. Mix well and shape into a narrow loaf. Refrigerate at least 8 hours or overnight. Cut into slices and fry in a skillet on both sides until brown.

Put the slices of meat close together in a roasting pan. Mix together the soup and water and spread over the meat slices.

Bake at 325° for 1 hour.

Porcupine Meatballs

½ cup uncooked white rice

1 lb. hamburger

1 small onion, finely minced

1 tsp. salt

½ tsp. pepper

½ cup water

1 8-oz. can tomato sauce

1 can tomato soup, plus 1 can water

2 tsp. Worcestershire sauce

Wash the rice and then combine it with the hamburger, onion, salt, pepper, and ½ cup water. Mix well and shape into balls the size of walnuts. Place them in a heavy oven-proof pot with a tight-fitting lid.

Mix together the tomato sauce, soup and water, and Worcestershire sauce and pour over the meatballs.

Cover and bake for 45 minutes; uncover and bake for 15 more minutes.

Notes:

Notes:

Pot Roast

1 boneless beef chuck roast (about 3 lb.)
6 T. flour, divided
6 T. butter, divided
3 cups hot water
2 tsp. beef bouillon granules
1 large onion, quartered
1 stalk celery, cut into pieces
1 tsp. salt
½ tsp. pepper
4 carrots, cut in quarters
4-6 potatoes, peeled and quartered

Sprinkle the roast with 1 T. flour. In a large Dutch oven or heavy pot, brown the roast on all sides in half of the butter. Add the water, bouillon, onion, celery, salt, and pepper and bring to a boil. Reduce heat; cover and simmer for 1 hour. Add carrots and potatoes, cover, and simmer 45-60 minutes or until the meat is tender and vegetables are cooked. Remove meat and vegetables to a serving platter and keep warm.

Strain cooking juices and set aside. In the Dutch oven, melt the remaining butter, stir in the remaining flour, and cook, stirring constantly, until bubbly. Add 2 cups of the cooking juices and blend until smooth. Cook, stirring constantly, until thickened; add additional cooking juices until the gravy is of desired consistency. Adjust seasoning to taste.

Wedding Meal Menu for 200 Guests

40 pans of chicken dressing

50 pounds of meat loaf

100 pounds of mashed potatoes

14 quarts of Amish bologna

30 pounds of cheese

8 gallons of noodles

6 gallons of gravy

15 gallons of broccoli salad

7 gallons of fresh fruit

40 dishes of Graham Cracker Fluff

25 pies

6 sheet cakes

5 gallons of ice cream

Quick and Easy Ranch Baked Beans

¼ cup oil
2 cups onions, chopped
1 lb. lean hamburger
1 tsp. salt
1 cup catsup
2 T. prepared mustard
2 tsp. cider vinegar
2 cans pork and beans
2 cans kidney beans, rinsed and drained
¼ cup brown sugar

Simmer onions in oil until golden. Add hamburger and cook until beef is browned. Add remainder of ingredients and stir to blend. Heat thoroughly. Pour into a casserole dish and bake at 400° for 30 minutes.

Ribbon Meat Loaf

1 lb. hamburger
¼ cup onion, chopped
salt and pepper to taste
2 eggs
dressing (see below)

Dressing

1½ cups bread cubes
beef stock to moisten
¼ cup chopped onion
a small amount of raisins (optional)
2 T. melted butter

Mix together the ingredients for the dressing and set aside.

Mix together the ingredients for the meat loaf, except for dressing, and spread one layer of the meat mixture in a greased

Notes:

Notes:

loaf pan. Put a layer of dressing over the meat layer. Alternate layers, ending with a meat layer. Press down so there are no gaps in the layers.

Bake at 350° for 1 hour and 15 minutes.

Rice Krispie Chicken

1 tsp. salt
½ tsp. pepper
½ cup butter, melted and slightly cooled
1 chicken, cut into pieces
2 cups Rice Krispies cereal, crushed

Mix the salt and pepper into the melted butter. Dip chicken pieces into the melted butter mixture and then roll in the Rice Krispies until well coated.

Arrange on a baking dish, skin side up, being careful not to crowd the pieces.

Bake uncovered at 350° for 1 hour or until done.

Rice Krispie Hamburger Bake

2 lb. hamburger
1 onion, chopped
6 cups Rice Krispies cereal
2 cans chicken and rice soup
2 cans cream of mushroom soup

Brown the hamburger and onion; drain off grease.

Mix all ingredients together and pour into a large casserole dish. Bake at 350° for 1 hour.

Scalloped Oysters

4 cups saltine crackers, coarsely crushed
1 10-oz. can oysters
powdered mustard (optional)
2 cups milk
1 egg, beaten
1 tsp. salt
pepper to taste
⅓ cup butter
paprika

Lightly butter a 1½ quart casserole dish. Place a layer of cracker crumbs on the bottom and then a layer of oysters. Sprinkle on some powdered mustard. Repeat these layers one more time.

Mix together the milk, egg, salt, and pepper. Pour over the oysters. Arrange the butter over the top in small pats. Sprinkle with paprika.

Set a pan of water on a lower shelf of the oven and preheat oven to 350°. Bake the scalloped oysters at 350° for about 45 minutes or until done.

Notes:

Oysters are one of the few luxuries that the Amish permit themselves and are featured in holiday dishes, especially at Christmastime.

Shepherd's Pie

1 small onion, chopped
2 T. butter
1½ cups cooked roast beef, diced
½ cup cooked carrots, diced
1 cup leftover roast gravy
¼ tsp. salt
dash of pepper
1 cup mashed potatoes
shredded Cheddar cheese to taste

Sauté onion in butter until golden. Add meat, carrots, gravy, and seasonings. Mix together and then pour into a greased baking dish. Cover with mashed potatoes and then top with shredded cheese.

Bake at 400° for 20 minutes or until potatoes are golden brown and heated through.

Notes:

Snitz and Knepp

1 quart snitz (dried apples)
3 lb. ham
3 T. brown sugar
2 cups flour
1 tsp. salt
¼ tsp. pepper
4 tsp. baking powder
1 egg, well beaten
3 T. melted butter
milk

Wash the dried apples and cover them with water to soak overnight.

Place the ham in a large pot and cover with water. Bring to a boil and then reduce and simmer until the ham is tender, about 2-3 hours. Add the snitz along with the water they soaked in and the brown sugar to the pot and return to a boil; reduce heat, cover the pot, and simmer for 1-1½ hours longer.

In a large bowl, sift together the flour, salt, pepper, and baking powder. Add the egg and melted butter and enough milk to make a stiff batter.

Uncover the pot and bring the liquid back to a boil; drop the batter by tablespoonfuls into the boiling liquid. Cover tightly and simmer for 15 minutes.

Slice the ham and place the slices in the center of a serving platter. Spoon the snitz and knepp around the ham slices and serve immediately.

Sour Cream Beef and Noodle Bake

1 8-oz. package egg noodles
1 lb. hamburger
½ cup onion, chopped
1 8-oz. can tomato sauce
1 tsp. salt
⅛ tsp. pepper
½ tsp. garlic salt
1 cup cottage cheese
1 cup sour cream
1 cup Cheddar cheese, shredded

Cook noodles according to package directions; drain. Brown meat and onion and pour off fat. Add to the pan the tomato sauce, salt, pepper, and garlic salt. Heat through.

In a large bowl, combine the cooked noodles, cottage cheese, and sour cream. Put half of this mixture in the bottom of a 1½ quart casserole dish. Add half the meat mixture. Repeat layers. Top with Cheddar cheese.

Bake at 350° for 30 minutes.

Super-Duper Noodle Casserole

1 package noodles
1 lb. hamburger
½ cup onion, chopped
2 T. butter
½ tsp. pepper
1 tsp. salt
1 can cream of mushroom soup
1 can cream of chicken soup
1 can tomato soup
potato chips

Cook noodles according to the package directions and drain.

Brown hamburger and onion together; drain off grease.

Mix together all ingredients except potato chips. Top with crushed potato chips and bake at 350° for 30 minutes.

Notes:

MAIN DISHES AND CASSEROLES

Notes:

Swiss Steak

1 T. dry mustard
1½ tsp. salt
¼ tsp. pepper
½ cup flour
3 lb. round steak, cut into serving-sized pieces
3 T. oil or shortening
1½ cups onion, sliced
2 carrots, diced
2 T. Worcestershire sauce
2 tsp. brown sugar
2 cups canned tomatoes, broken into small pieces

Mix together the mustard, salt, pepper, and flour. Dredge the steak pieces in the flour mixture and then brown in a skillet to which has been added the oil.

Place the browned steaks in a baking dish and top the meat with the onions, carrots, Worcestershire sauce, brown sugar, and tomatoes.

Cover and bake at 325° for 1-1½ hours or until everything is completely tender.

The Amish are allowed to use telephones when necessary, but they may not have one inside their home. Several families will get together to install and maintain a "public" phone inside a small building often built for that purpose. The rule is, you may use a telephone to conduct business or in an emergency, but it must be far enough away that you cannot hear it ringing from the house.

Tamale Pie Casserole

2 T. oil
1 onion, minced
1 clove garlic, minced
½ lb. hamburger
¼ lb. ground pork or unseasoned pork sausage
3 large tomatoes
½ tsp. salt
1¼ tsp. chili powder
¼ tsp. oregano
1 small can pitted sliced olives
1 can whole kernel corn, drained
1 egg
½ cup milk
½ cup cornmeal
3 T. flour
1 tsp. baking powder
1½ cup Cheddar cheese, shredded

Heat oil in a large frying pan. Add onion and garlic and cook until limp. Crumble in the beef and pork and brown meat. Drain off grease.

Skin and cut up tomatoes and add to the meat mixture. Cook about 15 minutes, adding a small quantity of water if it seems too dry. Add the seasonings, olives, and corn. Stir to combine.

Cornmeal Topping

Mix together the egg, milk, and cornmeal. Add the flour and baking powder and beat until smooth.

Pour the meat mixture into a greased casserole dish and top with the cornmeal topping. Sprinkle the cheese over the top and bake at 350° for 30-40 minutes.

Notes:

Notes:

Barn Raising Dinner Menu for 250

24 loaves of bread

5 pounds of butter

21 crocks of mashed potatoes

4 large roasting pans of beef and gravy

8 crocks of cooked and buttered carrots

3 crocks of pickled carrots and cucumbers

45 quart jars home-canned applesauce

12 crocks of sweet apple snitz and prunes

350 doughnuts

5 gallons of maple syrup

45 lemon drop pies

Tuna Casserole

1 can cream of celery soup
½ cup milk
3 cups cooked egg noodles
1 6½-oz. can tuna
½ cup mayonnaise
1 cup celery, chopped
⅓ cup onion, chopped
¼ cup bell pepper, chopped
½ tsp. salt
1 cup sharp Cheddar cheese, shredded

Blend the soup and milk together and then mix all ingredients except cheese together. Pour mixture into a casserole dish and sprinkle cheese over the top.

Bake uncovered at 425° for 20 minutes.

Tuna, Cheese, and Rice Muffins

2 cups cooked rice
1 cup Cheddar cheese, shredded
1 6½-oz. can tuna, drained
¾ cup black olives, sliced
2 T. milk
1 T. instant diced onions
1 T. parsley flakes
1 tsp. salt
2 eggs, beaten

Combine all ingredients and mix well. Grease muffin tins and divide tuna mixture evenly into cups.

Bake at 375° for 15 minutes or until lightly browned on top. Loosen with spatula and serve.

Tuna Macaroni Casserole

2 cups uncooked macaroni
2 T. salt
4 T. butter, melted
¼ cup milk
¾ cup Cheddar cheese, shredded
1 6½-oz. can tuna
1 cup cooked peas
¼ cup onion, chopped

Cook macaroni in 2 quarts water to which the salt has been added; boil for 8 minutes and then drain, but don't rinse. Place the macaroni and the rest of the ingredients in a large mixing bowl and mix well. Pour mixture into a buttered casserole dish and bake at 350° for 25 minutes or until thoroughly heated.

Tuna Stroganoff

2 small cans tuna
1 can cream of chicken soup
½ cup sour cream
¾ cup milk
2 T. chopped fresh parsley
¼ tsp. salt
pepper to taste
2 cups cooked egg noodles
2 tsp. melted butter
3 T. dry bread crumbs

Drain the tuna and fork it into small chunks. In a large bowl, blend the soup and sour cream and then stir in the milk. Add the tuna, parsley, salt, and pepper. Mix well. Add the cooked noodles and gently blend.

Mix together the melted butter and bread crumbs.

Pour the tuna mixture into a buttered casserole dish and top with the bread crumbs.

Bake at 350° for 20-25 minutes or until hot and bubbly.

Notes:

Tuna Swiss Pie

2 cans (6½ oz.) tuna, drained
1 cup Swiss cheese, shredded
½ cup green onion, chopped
½ cup mushrooms, sliced
1 9-inch pastry shell, baked
3 eggs
1 cup mayonnaise
½ cup milk

Mix together the tuna, cheese, onion, and mushrooms. Spoon into the pastry shell.

Beat eggs slightly and then add and blend the mayonnaise and milk with the eggs. Pour over tuna mixture in pastry shell.

Set pie plate on a cookie sheet lined with aluminum foil. Bake at 375° for 50 minutes or until an inserted knife comes out clean.

Turkey Supreme

2 cups turkey, cooked and diced (can substitute chicken)
2 cups uncooked macaroni
2 cups milk
2 cans cream of chicken soup
1 medium onion, chopped
½ tsp. salt
¼ tsp. pepper
3 T. butter, melted
1 cup Velveeta cheese, cut into small pieces

Combine all ingredients except Velveeta and pour into a greased casserole dish. Refrigerate for at least 8 hours or overnight. Remove from the refrigerator an hour or so before baking.

Bake at 350° for 1 hour. Top with Velveeta cheese and put back in the oven for another half hour, taking the casserole out of the oven and spreading the cheese over the top when it has melted and then returning to the oven to finish baking.

Wigglers

5 slices bacon, chopped
1½ lb. hamburger
1 onion, chopped
1 cup carrots, sliced
1 cup celery, chopped
2 cups potatoes, peeled and chopped
1½ cups cooked spaghetti noodles
2 cups peas
1 can cream of mushroom soup
salt and pepper to taste
3 cups tomato juice or soup
6 oz. Cheddar cheese, grated
butter

Cook bacon and set aside. In the same pan, brown hamburger and onions together; drain off grease. In 2 separate pots, cook vegetables and spaghetti until half done.

Mix everything together except the tomato juice, cheese, and butter. Place the mixture in a large roaster. Pour the tomato juice over everything, sprinkle on the cheese, and dot with butter. Bake at 350° for 1½ hours.

> The Holy Bible guides everyday life for the Amish. They believe in the doctrines of salvation: the sinful nature of man, the need for repentance and baptism of adults, the atonement of Christ, brotherly love, self-denial, nonresistance, and nonconformity.

Yum-a-Setta

2 lb. hamburger
salt and pepper to taste
2 T. brown sugar
¼ cup onion, chopped
1 can tomato soup
1 16-oz. package egg noodles
1 can cream of chicken soup
1 cup Velveeta cheese

Brown hamburger with salt, pepper, brown sugar, and onion; drain off grease. Add tomato soup to the meat mixture and mix.

This makes a great potluck dish.

Notes:

When an Amish person dies, their body is placed in a church-owned cemetery. All the headstones are uniform in size and style, but there may be a few markers that appear under the fence line at the edge of the cemetery. These are the markers of those church members who died while under the ban of shunning. The Amish believe that putting them under the fence allows God to decide if that person is inside or outside of the family of God.

Meanwhile, cook the egg noodles according to package directions; drain. Add cream of chicken soup to the noodles and mix.

Layer hamburger mixture and noodle mixture in a 13 x 9-inch casserole dish with Velveeta cheese between layers. Bake at 350° for 30 minutes.

DESSERTS

The Amish are well-known for their desserts—especially pies—and the assortment of recipes is astounding. Pastry-making is an acquired skill, and Amish girls learn early how to turn out a good pie. The trick to good crusts is to measure carefully and handle quickly and gently.

Amish church services last several hours, and for young children the seemingly endless sitting on backless church benches can be trying. Mothers know this, so sometime during the service a plate of cookies will be passed around for the youngsters. A cookie definitely helps to quietly pass the time.

*Do not be conformed to this world,
but be transformed by the renewing of your mind,
that you may prove what is that good and
acceptable and perfect will of God.*

Romans 12:2

Lord, Your words are sweeter than honey to me. Through Your precepts I gain understanding. Help me to not stray from the righteous path You have set before me and teach me Your judgments that I might live according to Your Word. As I place my hope in You, Lord, my heart rejoices. How sweet are Your words to me!

Amish Cottage Cheese Custard Pie

½ cup sugar
2 eggs
1 cup cottage cheese
½ tsp. salt
½ cup milk
½ cup heavy cream
1 unbaked pie shell
cinnamon

Beat together the sugar, eggs, and cottage cheese until very creamy. Stir in salt. Finally, add the milk and cream and stir to blend. Pour into the pie shell and sprinkle generously with cinnamon.

Bake at 450° for 25 minutes or until set in the middle.

Amish Date and Oatmeal Cake

1 cup boiling water
2 cups quick-cooking oats
¾ cup butter, softened to room temperature
2 cups brown sugar
2 eggs
1½ cups dates, finely chopped
1 cup pecans, coarsely chopped
1 tsp. grated orange rind
½ cup flour
1 tsp. baking soda
½ tsp. salt
1 tsp. nutmeg
1 tsp. allspice

In a large mixing bowl, pour boiling water over the oats and mix well; allow to cool slightly. Blend in the butter, brown sugar, eggs, dates, pecans, and orange rind.

Notes:

Amish women have their babies in the hospital, in birthing centers with midwives, and at home. When a *schnuck buply* (cute baby) is born, a *maut*, or hired girl, will stay at the home for up to six weeks to help the new mother, taking care of the home and other family members. *Mauts* are often teenage cousins or younger sisters of the new mom, and even though they are quite young, they are well able to keep the household running smoothly.

Notes:

Sift together the flour, baking soda, salt, nutmeg, and allspice and mix into the oat batter.

Pour the batter into a greased 8-inch square pan and bake at 350° for 45 minutes or until done (the cake will shrink away slightly from the sides of the pan). Cool to warm, cut into squares, and serve plain, with vanilla ice cream, or with whipped cream.

Amish No-Bake Cookies

½ cup butter
½ cup milk
2 cups sugar
3 T. unsweetened baking cocoa
½ cup peanut butter
1 tsp. vanilla
¼ tsp. salt
3 cups quick-cooking oats
½ cup pecans, chopped

In a small saucepan, combine the butter, milk, sugar, and cocoa. Bring to a boil, stirring, and boil for 1 minute. Remove from heat and stir in the peanut butter, vanilla, and salt. Mix in the oats and pecans.

Drop the dough by teaspoonfuls onto waxed paper and let stand at room temperature for 1 hour. Store in a container with a tight-fitting lid with waxed paper between the layers.

Amish Friendship Bread Starter

2¼ tsp. (1 package) active dry yeast
¼ cup warm water
3 cups flour, divided
3 cups sugar, divided
3 cups warm milk, divided

Do not use metal bowls or utensils.

Notes:

Day 1

In a small bowl, dissolve yeast in water. Let stand 10 minutes.

In a 2-quart glass, plastic, or ceramic container, or in a gallon freezer bag, combine 1 cup flour and 1 cup sugar. Mix thoroughly so when the milk is added the flour won't be lumpy. Slowly stir in 1 cup milk and the yeast mixture. If you are using a gallon freezer bag, seal tightly and squish the bag until thoroughly mixed. If using a bowl, once it's thoroughly mixed, cover loosely. Leave this mixture on a counter; do not refrigerate during the process of fermentation.

Days 2-4

Stir starter with a wooden spoon or squish bag daily. If you are using a bag, you can open the top to let out the air bubbles that will develop. (Sometimes I do this several times a day if there seems to be a lot of air inside the bag.)

Day 5

Stir in 1 cup flour, 1 cup sugar, and 1 cup milk. Stir or squish bag until everything is well incorporated.

Days 6-9

Stir starter with a wooden spoon or squish bag daily.

Day 10

Stir in 1 cup flour, 1 cup sugar, and 1 cup milk. Remove 2 cups starter to make your bread (recipe follows), divide the remainder into 1-cup portions to give to friends along with a copy of this recipe, or store excess in the refrigerator and begin the 10-day process over again.

Once you have made the starter, you will consider it Day 1 so you will ignore step 1 in this recipe and proceed directly to step 2. You can also freeze the starter in 1-cup measures for later use. Frozen starter will take at least 3 hours at room temperature to thaw before using.

Notes:

The Amish work from sunrise to sundown. When everyone else changes to daylight savings time, the Amish don't bother—this is "slow" time.

Amish Friendship Bread

1 cup starter
⅔ cup oil
3 eggs, beaten
½ cup milk
1 tsp. vanilla extract
2 cups flour
1 cup sugar
1½ tsp. baking powder
½ tsp. baking soda
½ tsp. salt
2 tsp. cinnamon
1 large package vanilla instant pudding mix
nuts, optional
raisins, optional
dates, optional
cinnamon sugar

In a large nonmetallic bowl, mix together the starter, oil, eggs, milk, and vanilla extract.

In a separate bowl, mix together the flour, sugar, baking powder, baking soda, salt, cinnamon, and vanilla instant pudding mix. Stir into the starter mixture and mix well. At this point, you can add nuts, raisins, or dates—use about 1 cup total.

Grease 2 loaf pans and sprinkle the bottoms liberally with a cinnamon and sugar mixture. Pour the batter into the loaf pans and sprinkle the top of bread also with cinnamon sugar.

Bake at 350° for 50-60 minutes or until a toothpick comes out clean. Cool in loaf pans for 10 minutes before turning out onto a wire rack to cool completely.

Amish Sugar Cookies

1 cup sugar
1 cup powdered sugar
1 cup butter
1 cup oil
2 eggs
1 tsp. vanilla
1 tsp. cream of tartar
4½ cups flour
1 tsp. baking soda

Combine sugars, butter, and oil and beat well. Add eggs and vanilla and beat again. Sift together dry ingredients and gradually add, mixing well after each addition.

Drop by teaspoonfuls onto cookie sheets and bake at 350° for about 8 minutes or until done.

Amish Vanilla Pie

1 egg
1 T. flour
½ cup brown sugar, packed
½ cup molasses or sorghum
1 cup water
1 tsp. vanilla
¼ tsp. mace
¼ tsp. salt
1 unbaked pastry shell
Crumb Topping (recipe follows)

In a medium saucepan, beat the egg until frothy. Blend in flour and add brown sugar, molasses, water, vanilla, mace, and salt. Mix well. Over medium heat, bring mixture just to full rolling boil, stirring often. Remove mixture from heat and set aside to cool and thicken slightly.

Place the pie plate with unbaked pastry on an oven rack. Pour filling into shell. Sprinkle Crumb Topping over the top of filling.

Notes:

This is a variation of Shoo-Fly Pie.

Notes:

The Amish do have mirrors in their homes, but they are usually quite small. If they have a larger mirror hung on a wall, it is often half covered with a piece of fabric, such as a small curtain. This ensures modesty and helps one resist the temptation to look at their reflection too often.

Bake at 350° for 45 minutes or until top is a deep golden brown. If the pastry starts browning too quickly, protect pastry edge with foil.

The filling will be a bit soft. Cool completely before cutting.

Crumb Topping

1 cup flour
½ cup brown sugar, packed
1 tsp. vanilla
½ tsp. cream of tartar
½ tsp. baking soda
¼ tsp. mace
¼ tsp. salt
¼ cup cold butter

In a medium mixing bowl, combine flour, brown sugar, vanilla, cream of tartar, baking soda, mace, and salt. Cut in the butter until mixture resembles coarse crumbles.

Amish Wedding Nothings

1 egg
¾ cup cream
pinch of salt
2-3 cups flour
shortening or lard for deep frying
powdered sugar for sprinkling

Beat the egg and then stir in the cream, salt, and enough flour to make a stiff dough. Divide the dough into 7 balls and roll each ball flat and very thin. Cut three 2-inch slits through the middle of the circle of dough.

Heat the shortening in a deep fryer to 365°. Fry one piece at a time, turning over with two forks when it turns a light golden color.

Take out when done and drain on paper towels. Sprinkle with powdered sugar. Stack nothings on top of each other, sprinkling with powdered sugar each time you add another to the stack.

Angel Food Cake

1⅔ cups egg whites

1 cup sugar

1 tsp. vanilla

1¼ cups cake flour

1⅓ cups powdered sugar

1½ tsp. cream of tartar

¼ tsp. salt

Beat egg whites until stiff peaks form. Gradually add sugar and vanilla.

Mix together flour, powdered sugar, cream of tartar, and salt. Add to egg whites a few tablespoons at a time, folding in thoroughly and carefully.

Pour the batter in an ungreased angel food tube pan and bake at 350° for 45-50 minutes or until done. Invert pan for one hour and then carefully loosen sides of cake to help release from the pan.

Apple Coffee Cake

1 can apple pie filling (either a quart of your home-canned or a store-bought 20-oz. can)

2 eggs

1 cup oil

2 cups flour

1 tsp. baking soda

1 tsp. vanilla

2 cups sugar

1 tsp. cinnamon

1 tsp. salt

1 cup nuts, chopped

Combine all ingredients in a large mixing bowl and mix well by hand. Pour batter into a greased 9 x 13-inch pan. (Optional: Before baking you can sprinkle top with some granulated or brown sugar.) Bake at 350° for 1 hour.

Notes:

You'll need 1½-2 dozen large eggs to yield 1⅔ cups of egg whites for this recipe.

You can save the yolks for future use by freezing them for up to four months in your freezer. But you will need to add either ½ tsp. salt or 1½ tsp. sugar (depending on your intended use—sweet or savory) before freezing. Gently stir the sugar or salt into four egg yolks and freeze in very clean ice cube trays or small freezer baggies, making sure to get as much air out as possible. If you use ice cube trays, transfer the frozen cubes to freezer baggies for long-term storage.

DESSERTS

Notes:

Apple Crisp

4 cups apples, pared and sliced
⅔ cup brown sugar
½ cup flour
½ cup oatmeal
⅓ cup butter, room temperature
¾ tsp. cinnamon
¾ tsp. nutmeg

Grease the bottom and sides of an 8-inch square baking pan. Spread apples in the pan. Stir together the remainder of ingredients until you make coarse crumbles. Sprinkle over apples.

Bake at 375° for 30 minutes or until apples are completely cooked and tender.

Apple Goodie

Filling

½ cup sugar
2 T. flour
¼ tsp. salt
1 tsp. cinnamon
1½ quarts (6 cups) apples, pared and sliced

Mix together all filling ingredients and press into a 9x13-inch baking pan.

Topping

1 cup oatmeal
1 cup brown sugar
1 cup flour
¼ tsp. baking soda
⅓ tsp. baking powder
½ cup butter

Mix dry ingredients and then cut in the butter until you have coarse crumbles. Spread over the top of the apple mixture and bake at 350° for 35-40 minutes or until golden brown on top.

Applesauce Half-Moon Pies

Pie crust, double batch
1 quart applesauce
1 egg white, beaten well
cinnamon sugar

Roll out bits of pie crust to make circles about 5 inches across. Just off the center of circle, place some applesauce and fold crust over. Crimp edges well, using a fork and a bit of water to help seal edges. Brush tops with beaten egg white and then sprinkle with cinnamon sugar. Place on an ungreased cookie sheet.

Bake at 375° until done, about 25 minutes.

Applesauce Spice Cake

2½ cups flour
2 cups sugar
1½ tsp. salt
1½ tsp. baking soda
¼ tsp. baking powder
¾ tsp. cinnamon
½ tsp. cloves
½ tsp. allspice
2 cups applesauce
½ cup shortening
½ cup water
3 eggs
1 cup raisins
½ cup chopped nuts

In a mixing bowl, sift together flour, sugar, salt, baking soda, baking powder, cinnamon, cloves, and allspice. Add applesauce, shortening, and water; beat 2 minutes. Add eggs and beat 2 minutes more. Stir in raisins and nuts. Pour batter into 2 greased and floured loaf pans.

Bake at 350° for 55-60 minutes.

Notes:

Notes:

Get on your knees and thank God you're on your feet.

Baked Apples

1 cup sugar
½ cup flour
1 tsp. cinnamon
1 cup brown sugar
1 cup water
2 tsp. butter
4 or more cooking apples, depending on size

Combine all ingredients except for apples and boil, stirring often, until thickened.

Peel apples, core, and cut in half. Place cut side up in a 9 x 13-inch baking pan. Pour thickened sugar mixture over apples and bake at 350° for 30-45 minutes or until apples are soft.

Berry Dumplings

Berry mixture
¾ cup sugar
1 quart water
1½ tsp. lemon juice
⅓ tsp. salt
1½ quarts fresh blackberries, loganberries, marionberries, etc.

Dumplings
2¼ cups flour
⅛ tsp. salt
1½ tsp. sugar
3 tsp. baking powder
1 cup milk
1 tsp. vanilla
½ cup water
2½ T. butter, melted

In a large pot with a tight-fitting lid, mix together the sugar, water, lemon juice, and salt. Heat on medium-low heat until sugar is melted and then add berries. Cover and simmer for 10 minutes.

Mix together the dumpling ingredients by first blending together the dry ingredients and then adding the liquids. Blend until smooth. Spoon batter on the berries and simmer for 25 minutes longer, keeping the lid on tightly for the entire time.

Serve berries ladled over dumplings in bowls while still warm.

Black and Blue(berry) Cobbler

1 cup sugar, divided
1 cup flour
2 T. baking powder
¼ tsp. salt
½ cup milk
1 tsp. vanilla
1 T. melted butter or oil
1 cup blackberries or blueberries or a combination of the two
¾ cup boiling water

In a medium mixing bowl, mix together ½ cup sugar, flour, baking powder, and salt. Stir in the milk, vanilla, and butter or oil and mix well. Spread batter in a buttered 10 x 6-inch baking dish. Scatter berries on top of dough; sprinkle with ½ cup sugar (more or less depending on taste). Pour boiling water over all.

Bake at 375° (350° if using a glass baking dish) for 25-30 minutes or until done.

Notes:

Notes:

Bread Pudding

2 cups milk (use whole milk or thin cream)
¼ cup butter
⅔ cup sugar (you can use granulated or brown sugar, depending on taste)
3 eggs
2 tsp. cinnamon
¼ tsp. nutmeg
1 tsp. vanilla
3 cups bread, torn into small pieces
½ cup raisins (optional)

In a medium saucepan, heat milk just until film forms over the top. Add the butter and stir until butter is melted. Cool to lukewarm.

Beat together sugar, eggs, cinnamon, nutmeg, and vanilla. Continue beating and gradually add milk mixture.

Place torn bread in a buttered 1½ quart casserole dish. Sprinkle with raisins if using. Pour milk mixture on top of bread and bake at 350° for 45-50 minutes or until done. Serve warm either plain or with whipped cream or caramel sauce.

Butter Crust Pastry

1 cup flour
½ tsp. salt
½ cup cold butter
2 T. cold water

Combine the flour and salt and then cut in the butter until the mixture is the size of small peas. Sprinkle on 2 T. or more of cold water. Blend with a fork just until dough comes together, forming a ball. Turn out on a floured surface and roll crust ⅛-inch thick. This is enough to make one single crust.

Buttermilk Pie

2 cups sugar
1 T. flour
½ cup butter, melted
3 eggs, beaten
pinch of baking soda
1 cup buttermilk
1 tsp. lemon juice
1 unbaked pie shell

Combine the sugar and flour. Add the melted butter, blending well. Add the beaten eggs, blending well again. Combine baking soda and buttermilk, and then add that to the mixture. Stir in the lemon juice and mix thoroughly.

Pour into the unbaked pie shell and bake at 375° for 40-45 minutes or until done.

Busy Day Cobbler

½ cup butter
1½ cups sugar
1 cup flour
¾ cup milk
¼ tsp. salt
1½ tsp. baking powder
1 20-oz. can fruit plus liquid
sugar or cinnamon sugar

Place butter in a 9-inch square baking pan and put in a 350° oven to melt.

Meanwhile, beat other ingredients, except fruit, together until smooth. Pour over melted butter; don't stir. Next, pour can of fruit and juice over the batter; don't stir. Sprinkle top with ½ cup sugar (or cinnamon sugar) and bake at 350° for 30-45 minutes.

Notes:

Notes:

Cake Pie

1 cup sugar
¼ cup butter or shortening
½ cup milk
1 egg, beaten
1 cup flour
1 tsp. baking powder
½ tsp. vanilla
4 T. baking cocoa
½ cup sugar
6 T. water
¼ tsp. vanilla
1 unbaked pie crust

Top Part

Cream together the 1 cup sugar and butter or shortening. In a separate bowl, mix together the milk and egg; in another bowl, sift together the flour and baking powder. Alternately add the milk mixture and flour mixture to the sugar and butter, mixing well after each addition. Add the ½ tsp. vanilla and mix well. Set aside while making the lower part.

Lower Part

Mix together the cocoa, ½ cup sugar, water, and ¼ tsp. vanilla. Pour this lower part into an unbaked pie shell. Over this pour the top part. The chocolate will come up around the outside edge.

Bake at 350° for 35 minutes or until set and toothpick comes out clean.

Carmel-Apple Dumplings

2 cups brown sugar

3 cups water

¼ tsp. cinnamon

½ tsp. nutmeg

2 cups flour

1 tsp. salt

2 tsp. baking powder

¼ cup butter

¾ cup shortening

½ cup milk

6 apples, peeled and cored but left whole

Caramel Sauce

In a medium saucepan, combine the brown sugar, water, cinnamon, and nutmeg. Bring to a boil and boil for 10 minutes. Set aside.

Dough

In a mixing bowl, combine the flour, salt, and baking powder. With a pastry cutter, cut in the butter and shortening. Add the milk and mix to form a dough ball.

Roll out pieces of dough and wrap around the apples. Place in a baking dish. Pour sauce over apples and bake at 375° for 35 minutes or until apples are tender.

Notes:

Idleness is the nest in which mischief lays its eggs.

Notes:

Carmel Popcorn

1 cup butter
2 cups brown sugar, packed
½ cup (plus a bit more) light Karo syrup
1 tsp. salt
1 tsp. baking soda
1 tsp. vanilla
6 quarts popped corn

Bring the butter, brown sugar, Karo syrup, and salt to a boil over medium heat, stirring the whole time. Remove the saucepan from the heat and stir in baking soda and vanilla. Immediately pour over popcorn, stirring to evenly coat.

Turn popcorn into 2 or more large roasting pans. Bake at 250° for 1 hour, stirring every 15 minutes. Turn out onto waxed paper and allow to cool.

Carmel Pudding

2 T. butter
¾ cup brown sugar
1 quart milk
2 eggs
2 T. cornstarch
2 T. flour
pinch of salt
¼ cup milk

Melt the butter in a heavy saucepan. Add brown sugar and stir until bubbly and brown, being careful not to burn it. Stir in the milk, heat thoroughly, and then set aside.

Beat together the eggs, cornstarch, flour, salt, and ¼ cup milk. Add to the warm milk and brown sugar mixture and stir just until it reaches the boiling point. Remove from heat and beat with a rotary beater. Let the pudding cool a bit before eating.

Carrot Cake with Cream Cheese Frosting

2 cups flour
2 cups brown sugar
1 tsp. salt
2 tsp. cinnamon
2 tsp. baking soda
4 eggs
1½ cups oil
2 cups grated carrots
½ cup butter, softened
1 large package cream cheese, softened
1 box powdered sugar
3 tsp. vanilla
2 cups chopped walnuts

Cake

Mix together the flour, brown sugar, salt, cinnamon, and baking soda. Add eggs and oil and blend thoroughly. Add grated carrots and mix well. Pour batter into a greased 9 x 13-inch baking dish and bake at 350° for 30 minutes. Allow cake to cool before frosting.

Frosting

Meanwhile, prepare frosting. Cream together the butter, cream cheese, powdered sugar, and vanilla until smooth and creamy. Frost the cooled carrot cake and scatter the walnuts over the top.

Notes:

Notes:

Cherry Pie

4 cups canned pitted cherries, undrained

3 T. sugar

2 T. Clear Jel (similar to cornstarch)

½ tsp. red food coloring

½ tsp. apple cider vinegar

2 unbaked pie crusts, one for the pie itself and one for the top crust

In a large saucepan, combine the cherries with their liquid, sugar, Clear Jel, food coloring, and vinegar. Heat, stirring, until mixture thickens. Pour into the pie shell, top with the other crust, making sure to cut holes to vent or use a lattice of dough strips.

Bake in a 400° oven for 10 minutes, then reduce heat to 350° and continue baking for 40-45 minutes longer.

Chocolate Chip Cookies for a Crowd

Makes 30 dozen cookies

6 cups butter

3 cups sugar

4½ cups brown sugar

6 eggs

12 tsp. vanilla

14½ cups flour

6 tsp. baking soda

2 tsp. salt

48 oz. chocolate chips (4 cups)

In a large mixing bowl, cream together the butter, sugar, and brown sugar. Add the eggs and vanilla and beat again. Sift together the flour, baking soda, and salt and blend into the butter and sugar mixture. Stir in the chocolate chips.

Place rounded teaspoonfuls of dough on ungreased cookie sheets and bake at 350° for 8-10 minutes.

Chocolate Chip Pie

½ cup butter
1 cup chocolate chips
1 cup sugar
½ cup flour
2 eggs
1½ tsp. vanilla
1 cup pecans, chopped
1 unbaked pie shell

In a double boiler, melt the butter and chocolate chips, stirring until well blended. Remove from heat and cool. Add sugar and flour and mix well. Combine the eggs and vanilla and beat well; add to the chocolate mixture. Stir in nuts and pour into the pie shell.

Bake at 350° for 35-40 minutes or until set. Great served warm with vanilla ice cream or with whipped cream on top.

Chocolate Cornstarch Pudding

⅔ cup sugar
¼ cup cornstarch
3 T. cocoa powder
¼ tsp. salt
2¾ cups milk
2 T. butter

In a medium saucepan, stir together the sugar, cornstarch, cocoa powder, and salt. Gradually add the milk, stirring constantly, to blend. Turn on heat and bring mixture to a boil over medium heat, stirring constantly. Boil for 1 minute. Remove from heat and add the butter.

Notes:

A good remedy for burns is to immediately swab egg white onto the area; it takes the burn away.

Notes:

Chocolate Frosting

½ cup butter, softened
4 cups powdered sugar
1 egg white
1 tsp. vanilla
pinch of salt
3 squares (3 oz. total) unsweetened baking chocolate, melted

In a large mixing bowl, combine all the ingredients and beat until thoroughly blended and smooth. If the frosting is too thick, add a small amount of hot water and blend again.

Chocolate Fudge

3 6-oz. packages chocolate chips
1 14-oz. can sweetened condensed milk
small pinch salt
1½ tsp. vanilla
½ cup chopped nuts

In a heavy saucepan over low heat, melt the chocolate chips with the sweetened condensed milk. Remove from heat and then stir in the remaining ingredients.

Spread evenly into a waxed-paper-lined 8-inch square pan. Chill 3 hours or until firm. Turn out fudge onto a cutting board, peel off waxed paper, and cut into squares. Store loosely covered at room temperature.

Chocolate Sauerkraut Cake

1 16-oz. can sauerkraut, rinsed and well drained
⅔ cup butter
1½ cups sugar
3 eggs
2 tsp. vanilla
½ cup unsweetened baking cocoa powder
1 tsp. baking powder
1 tsp. salt
1 tsp. baking soda
2¼ cups flour
1 cup cold water

Using your hands, squeeze out as much moisture from the kraut as possible. Chop it finely and set aside.

In a large mixing bowl, beat together the butter and sugar until light and fluffy. Add the eggs, one at a time, beating well after each addition. Add the vanilla, cocoa powder, baking powder, salt, and baking soda; blend well. Add the flour alternately with the water. Fold in the sauerkraut until well incorporated.

Pour into a greased 13 x 9-inch baking pan and bake at 350° for 30 minutes or until done. When cool frost with chocolate frosting, or cut when slightly warm and serve with whipped cream.

Notes:

Every year my father would buy handmade fruitcake from the Trappist monks. I knew it was meant to be a special treat, but I didn't care for it. After many years I found the courage to tell my father, and he laughed and said he didn't like fruitcake either, but he felt Christmas wouldn't be complete without it. Fortunately, Christmas Cake makes a great, tasty stand-in for the more traditional recipe.

Christmas Cake

1 lb. butter
1 lb. light brown sugar
6 eggs
4 cups flour, sifted
1 tsp. baking powder
2 T. nutmeg
½ cup orange juice
3 cups chopped pecans
1 lb. pale yellow seedless raisins

Cream together the butter and sugar. Add the eggs, 2 at a time, and beat until very light and mixture doesn't look grainy (takes about 20-25 minutes total). Sift together the flour, baking powder, and nutmeg. Add gradually to the creamed mixture and beat until well blended. Stir in the orange juice or blend in using lowest speed on mixer. Fold in the pecans and raisins.

Pour the cake batter into a 10-inch tube pan that has been greased and floured.

Bake at 300° for 1 hour and 45 minutes.

Remove from oven and cool for 10 minutes. Then turn the pan over and let cake slip out gently. Cool completely. Wrap tightly and store for at least a week before serving because it tends to be crumbly when fresh.

Christmas Sugar Cookies

½ cup butter
1 cup sugar
1 egg
1 tsp. vanilla
2¼ cups flour, sifted
½ tsp. salt
½ tsp. baking soda
¾ tsp. baking powder

Thoroughly cream together the butter and sugar. Add the egg and vanilla and beat again well.

Sift together the flour, salt, baking soda, and baking powder. Mix together thoroughly and chill at least 2-3 hours.

On a lightly floured surface, roll out dough ⅛-inch thick and cut into desired shapes. Bake at 325° for about 8-10 minutes. If your oven is too hot, even just a little, the cookies will brown too quickly around the edges.

Cool completely and then frost as desired.

Notes:

An old timer is someone who remembers when charity was a virtue—not an organization.

Notes:

Coffee Cake

1¼ cups flour
½ cup sugar
2 tsp. baking powder
½ tsp. salt
½ cup milk
1 egg, beaten
3 T. butter, melted and cooled

Topping

1 cup brown sugar, firmly packed
1 cup chopped nuts
1 T. flour
1 T. softened butter
2 tsp. cinnamon

In a bowl, stir together the flour, sugar, baking powder, and salt. Mix together the milk, egg, and butter. Pour the milk mixture all at once into the dry ingredients and stir just until moistened. Pour batter into a greased 8-inch square baking pan.

Mix together the topping ingredients and sprinkle over the top of the batter.

Bake in a preheated 375° oven for 20-25 minutes.

Crackletop Molasses Cookies

4 cups flour
2 T. unsweetened baking cocoa powder
2 tsp. baking soda
1½ tsp. cinnamon
½ tsp. cloves
½ tsp. salt
¾ cup butter, softened
1¼ cups sugar, divided
1 cup molasses

Mix together the flour, cocoa, baking soda, cinnamon, cloves, and salt.

In a large bowl, beat together the butter and 1 cup sugar until fluffy. Beat in molasses. Gradually add flour mixture and beat just until mixed. Divide dough in half. Pat each half into a flattened 1-inch-thick round. Wrap in plastic wrap and chill at least 1 hour.

Heat oven to 375° and lightly grease cookie sheets. Form tablespoonfuls of dough into 1-inch balls; roll in remaining ¼ cup sugar. Place one inch apart on prepared cookie sheets. Bake 10 minutes. Cool on cookie sheet for 1 minute before removing cookies to a rack to cool completely.

Cream Cheese Bars

⅓ cup butter
1 cup sugar, divided
1½ cups graham cracker crumbs
3 8-oz. packages cream cheese
4 eggs, beaten
1 tsp. vanilla
1 can blueberry pie filling (or a quart jar of home-canned pie filling)

In a saucepan, heat the butter and ¼ cup of the sugar until melted, stirring occasionally. Remove from heat and add graham

Notes:

cracker crumbs. Press mixture into the bottom of a 9 x 13-inch baking pan.

With an electric mixer, beat cream cheese until smooth. Gradually beat in remaining sugar (¾ cup). Add eggs one at a time, blending after each addition. Add vanilla and blend well.

Spoon blueberry pie filling over crust. Carefully pour cream cheese mixture over blueberry filling.

Bake until set, about 45 to 60 minutes. Chill and then cut into squares.

Cream Puffs

1 cup water
½ cup butter
1 tsp. sugar
¼ tsp. salt
1 cup flour, sifted
4 eggs
whipped cream

Heat the water, butter, sugar, and salt to a full rolling boil in a large saucepan. Add the flour all at once. Stir vigorously with a wooden spoon until mixture forms a thick, smooth ball that leaves the sides of the pan clean, about 1 minute. Remove from heat. Add the eggs, one at a time, beating well after each addition with wooden spoon, or until paste is shiny and smooth. Shape into puffs and bake at 425° for 15 minutes; reduce heat to 375° and bake for 5 more minutes. Cut a slash in the lower side of each puff and continue baking for 10 minutes or until puffs are firm, dry to the touch, and golden brown. Cool on a wire rack; cut tops off, fill with sweetened whipped cream, place tops back on top of the whipped cream, and serve.

Easy Coconut Macaroons

2⅔ cups shredded coconut
⅔ cup sweetened condensed milk
1 tsp. vanilla

In large bowl, combine all ingredients and mix well. Drop by teaspoonfuls one inch apart on a well-greased cookie sheet, pressing down the ends of coconut that stick up with the back of a spoon.

Bake at 350° for 10-12 minutes. Cool on rack.

Fresh Peach Pie

2 cups sliced fresh peaches
1 T. lemon juice
¼ cup sugar
3 T. cornstarch
2 tsp. butter
small pinch of salt
½ tsp. vanilla
1 9-inch pie shell, baked and cooled

Sprinkle peaches with lemon juice and sugar; let stand one hour. Drain and reserve liquid; there should be 1 cup syrup. Place syrup in a medium saucepan and add the cornstarch and mix well. Cook over low heat until thick, stirring constantly. Remove from heat; add butter, salt, and vanilla. Cool.

Place the peaches in the baked pie shell. Pour the cooled syrup over the peaches. Chill. Pipe with sweetened whipped cream or serve with vanilla ice cream.

Notes:

Notes:

Funeral Pie

In the past, raisins were one of the least expensive fruits you could buy, so Funeral Pie was (and still is) usually served after funerals as a way to remind mourners that they came into the world with nothing, and leave the world the same way. What's important is a life characterized by humility and faith in God.

Funeral Pie

1 double-crust pie pastry, unbaked
2 cups raisins
2 cups water, divided
½ cup brown sugar
½ cup granulated sugar
3 T. cornstarch
1½ tsp. cinnamon
¼ tsp. allspice
pinch of salt
1 T. cider vinegar
3 T. butter

Line a pie pan with half the pastry and set in refrigerator to chill.

Place the raisins and ⅔ cup of the water in a saucepan and heat over medium heat for 5 minutes.

Combine sugars, cornstarch, cinnamon, allspice, and salt in a bowl and, while constantly mixing, slowly add the remaining water. Add this mixture to the heating raisins. Cook and stir this until the mixture begins to bubble. Add the vinegar and butter and heat just until the butter is melted. Remove from heat and allow mixture to cool a bit. Pour into the prepared pie shell and top with the second crust.

Bake for 25 minutes at 400° or until golden. The pie will set up more as it cools.

Ginger Cake

2 eggs
1 tsp. baking soda
1 T. ground ginger
¼ cup butter, softened
1 cup boiling water
½ cup sugar
1 cup molasses
2¼ cups flour

Mix together all ingredients until well blended. Pour batter into a greased 9 x 9-inch baking pan and bake at 350° until done, about 30 minutes.

Ginger Cookies

½ cup butter
1 cup brown sugar, packed
1 egg
1 cup molasses
½ cup cream or evaporated milk
5 cups flour
1 tsp. baking soda
1 tsp. ginger
1 tsp. cinnamon
½ tsp. cloves
½ tsp. allspice
½ tsp. salt
Sugar Glaze (recipe follows)

Mix together thoroughly the butter, brown sugar, egg, molasses, and cream. Sift together the flour and spices and stir into the molasses mixture. Chill dough at least 2 hours.

Roll out ⅛-inch thick, using as little flour as possible. Cut into desire shapes. Place one inch apart on lightly greased cookie sheet. Bake at 375° for 8-10 minutes. Glaze with Sugar Glaze.

Notes:

If you see someone without a smile today, give him one of yours.

DESSERTS

Notes:

Sugar Glaze

1½ cups powdered sugar
2-3 T. water

Mix together until well blended and to desired consistency.

Graham Cracker Fluff

2 eggs, separated; whites stiffly beaten
⅔ cup milk
½ cup sugar
1 pkg. unflavored gelatin
½ cup cold water
1 cup cream, whipped
1 tsp. vanilla
3 T. butter, melted
12 graham crackers, crushed
3 T. sugar

In a double boiler, cook, stirring constantly, the egg yolks, milk, and ½ cup sugar until slightly thickened. Remove from heat.

Dissolve gelatin in cold water and then add to hot mixture. Cool until mixture begins to thicken.

Gently blend together the beaten egg whites, whipped cream, and vanilla and then gently fold into the egg yolk and gelatin mixture.

Mix together the melted butter, graham cracker crumbs, and 3 T. sugar. Sprinkle a small amount of the graham cracker crumb mixture in the bottom of a serving bowl. Add the fluff and then sprinkle the remainder of the crumbs over the top.

You can double or triple this recipe. A doubled recipe fits in a 9 x 13-inch pan and a tripled recipe fits a 10 x 14-inch pan.

Hunt Pies

10 cups flour
¼ tsp. salt
¼ tsp. baking powder
16 heaping T. shortening
3 cups milk
Home-canned or store-bought applesauce
cinnamon sugar

Mix together everything but the applesauce. Knead until dough forms a ball and then turn out on floured surface and roll out dough a bit at a time, making sure it's thin. Cut into circles or squares so that finished size will be approximately 3 x 5 inches or so. Place a good dollop of applesauce on one side of the dough and fold other half over the top. Crimp edges. Place on ungreased cookie sheets. Sprinkle with cinnamon sugar. Bake at 375° for 30 minutes or so until pastry is browned and crisp and looks done.

Lemon Butterceam Frosting

½ cup butter, softened
1 tsp. grated lemon rind
1 tsp. vanilla
pinch of salt
3½ cups powdered sugar
¼ cup milk
1 T. lemon juice

In a large mixing bowl, cream together the butter, lemon rind, vanilla, and salt until light and fluffy. Add the powdered sugar alternately with the milk and beat until creamy and smooth, beating well after each addition. Beat in the lemon juice.

Notes:

Hunt Pies are the perfect treat for hunting camp. They hold up well under rough conditions.

DESSERTS

Notes:

Lemon Meringue Pie

1 9-inch baked pie shell
1½ cups sugar, divided
⅓ cup cornstarch
1½ cups cold water
3 eggs, separated
3 T. butter
4 T. lemon juice
¼ tsp. cream of tartar
½ tsp. vanilla

Lemon Filling

In a saucepan, mix together ½ cup of sugar and the cornstarch. Gradually stir in the cold water. Cook over moderate heat, stirring constantly, until mixture thickens and bubbles. Boil 1 minute. Slowly stir half of this mixture into 3 slightly beaten egg yolks (save the whites for the meringue). Then beat this mixture into the hot mixture in the saucepan. Boil 1 minute longer, stirring constantly. Remove from heat. Continue stirring until smooth. Blend in the butter and lemon juice. Pour into the baked pie shell.

Meringue

Beat together the egg whites with cream of tartar and vanilla until frothy. Gradually beat in the rest of the sugar, one tablespoon at a time. Continue beating until the meringue is stiff and glossy.

Pile the meringue onto pie filling, being careful to seal edges onto the crust to prevent weeping. Pull up points in the meringue for decoration.

Bake at 350° for 8-10 minutes or until meringue is lightly browned. Cool and serve. Best if served the same day.

Lemon Sponge Pudding

¼ cup butter, softened
¾ cup sugar
3 eggs, separated
⅓ cup lemon juice
⅓ cup flour
1 T. lemon rind
¼ tsp. salt
1½ cups milk
small pinch cream of tartar
small pinch salt
powdered sugar

In a large bowl cream together butter and sugar. Beat in egg yolks, one at a time, beating well after each addition. Add lemon juice, flour, lemon rind, and salt, a bit at a time, beating well after each addition. Add milk in a stream while beating, and combine the mixture well.

In another bowl beat 3 egg whites with the pinch of cream of tartar and salt until they hold stiff peaks. Stir a quarter of the egg whites into the lemon mixture until thoroughly blended and then gently fold in the remainder of the egg whites.

Place pudding in a buttered soufflé or casserole dish. Set dish in a deep pan and add enough boiling water to the larger pan to reach halfway up the sides of the soufflé dish.

Bake in a preheated 350° oven for 50 minutes.

Sift powdered sugar over the top and serve warm or chilled. The sponge will separate, forming a custard-like sauce on the bottom.

Notes:

To get rid of sugar ants, place some mint jelly in a jar lid or a small saucer. It kills them as they carry it back to their nest.

DESSERTS

Notes:

When baking an empty pie crust, put a cup of raw white rice or small white beans into the bottom of the crust and then bake. The rice (or beans) will weight the bottom so the crust doesn't puff up while baking. Save your rice or beans in a marked container for future use when baking pie crusts.

Mama's Pie Crust

For Single Crust

1½ cup sifted flour

½ tsp. salt

½ cup shortening or lard

For Double Crust

2 cups sifted flour

1 tsp. salt

⅔ cup shortening or lard

In a teacup or small bowl, make a paste with ¼ cup of the above flour (⅓ cup if making double crust) and 3 T. water (¼ cup water for double crust). Set in refrigerator. Add salt to the remaining flour and cut shortening into the flour until the size of small peas. Add the flour and water paste and mix just until dough comes together. Form into a ball and turn out on a floured surface. Roll crust ⅛-inch thick.

Bake at 425° for 12-15 minutes.

Minted Nuts

1 cup sugar

½ cup water

1 generous T. corn syrup

⅛ tsp. salt

8 marshmallows

½ tsp. essence of peppermint

4 cups walnuts, broken

6 drops green food coloring

Cook slowly together the sugar, water, corn syrup, and salt. Cook until temperature reaches 230° on a candy thermometer. Turn heat off but leave pan over the hot burner and add food coloring and marshmallows. Stir until melted. Add peppermint and nuts. Stir with a circular motion until every nut is coated and the mixture hardens (takes about 5 minutes).

Cool on unglazed paper (paper bags are good). These minted nuts can be kept fresh in tightly covered jars for at least a week.

Mix-in-the-Pan Chocolate Cake

1½ cups flour
1 cup sugar
4 T. baking cocoa
1 tsp. baking soda
1 tsp. salt
6 T. oil
½ tsp. vanilla
1 T. vinegar
1 cup cold water

In an 8-inch square baking pan, mix together with a fork the flour, sugar, baking cocoa, baking soda, and salt.

In a separate bowl, mix together the oil, vanilla, vinegar, and cold water. Pour all at once into the baking pan with the flour mixture and blend with the fork until thoroughly blended together.

Bake at 350° for 35-40 minutes or until a toothpick inserted in the center of the cake comes out clean.

This cake is best eaten fresh and slightly warm from the oven. It's very good with whipped cream or vanilla ice cream.

Never-Fail Pie Crust

2 cups flour
½ tsp. salt
⅔ cup shortening
2 tsp. cider vinegar
1 egg
3½ T. very cold water

In a medium mixing bowl, combine the flour and salt. Cut in the shortening with a pastry blender or two knives until the mixture resembles coarse crumbs.

In a separate bowl, blend together the vinegar, egg, and water. Make a well in the center of the flour mixture, pour the vinegar mixture in the well, and stir until blended.

The addition of vinegar to this pastry dough results in a soft and moist crust, and the vinegar helps the crust remain pliable and light even if the dough is overworked.

Work the dough into a ball and then divide into two smaller balls. On a lightly floured surface, roll out each ball into a circle big enough to fit your pie plates with about 1-1½ inches draping over the sides. Transfer the dough to your pie plates by rolling it around your rolling pin and then unrolling dough over the pie plate. Crimp edges.

To bake, prick the bottom of the pastry with a fork. Bake at 425° for 10-15 minutes or until the crust is golden.

Nut Balls

⅔ cup butter
1 cup ground nut meats
1 cup flour
3 T. sugar
1 tsp. vanilla
pinch of salt
powdered sugar

Place all ingredients except powdered sugar in a bowl and work with fingers until well blended. Shape into balls the size of large marbles and place on ungreased cookie sheet or jelly roll pan.

Bake at 375° for 10 minutes. While still warm, roll in powdered sugar.

Old-Fashioned Custard Pie

½ cup sugar
1 tsp. vanilla
3 eggs
2 cups milk
⅛ tsp. salt
nutmeg
1 unbaked pie shell

Combine all the ingredients except for the nutmeg and mix

This is a tried-and-true recipe that you can quickly make when you want to serve something delicious and don't have a lot in the pantry. Custard pie is tasty simplicity.

thoroughly for several minutes. Pour the mixture into the unbaked pie shell and sprinkle generously with nutmeg.

Bake at 450° for 10 minutes. Reduce heat to 350° and bake another 30 minutes or until the center tests done.

Orange Frosted Cookies

⅔ cup shortening

¾ cup sugar

1 egg

½ cup orange juice

2 T. grated orange rind (optional)

2 cups flour

½ tsp. baking powder

½ tsp. baking soda

½ tsp. salt

Cookies

Mix together shortening, sugar, and egg. Stir in orange juice and rind. Sift together the flour, baking powder, baking soda, and salt. Add to creamed mixture and mix well.

Drop dough by rounded teaspoonfuls about 2 inches apart on an ungreased cookie sheet. Bake at 400° for 8-10 minutes. Cool and then frost.

Orange Butter Frosting

2½ T. butter, softened

1½ cups powdered sugar, sifted

1½ T. orange juice

Blend together the softened butter and powdered sugar. Stir in orange juice and blend until smooth. When cookies are cooled, frost with a swirl of frosting on top.

Notes:

> Adopt the pace of nature; her secret is patience.

Peach Custard Pie

6 peaches, pared and sliced
1 unbaked pie shell
¼ cup flour
¾ cup sugar
1 cup heavy cream

Filling

Arrange peaches in pie shell. Mix together the ¼ cup flour and ¾ cup sugar and then add cream. Blend thoroughly. Pour over peaches.

Topping

⅓ cup flour
⅓ cup sugar
3 T. butter

Combine the ⅓ cup flour, ⅓ cup sugar, and butter and mix until the size of coarse peas. Sprinkle over pie filling.

Bake at 425° for 10 minutes and then reduce heat to 350° and continue baking until custard is set, approximately 30 minutes.

Peanut Brittle

2 cups sugar
1 cup light Karo syrup
1 cup water
½ tsp. salt
2 cups peanuts
2 T. butter
2 tsp. baking soda

In a heavy 3-quart saucepan, heat and stir sugar, Karo syrup, and water until the sugar dissolves. Add salt. Cook over medium heat. When the temperature reaches 250° (use a candy thermometer), add the peanuts. Continue cooking, stirring, to hard crack stage (290°). Remove from heat.

Quickly stir in the butter and baking soda. Beat to a froth for a few seconds. Pour at once onto 2 well-buttered jelly roll pans, spreading with a spatula. Work quickly. Break up peanut brittle when set and completely cool.

Pear Pudding Cake

1 cup flour
⅔ cup sugar
1½ tsp. baking powder
½ tsp. cinnamon
¼ tsp. salt
small pinch of cloves
½ cup milk
2 cups chopped pears (skinned)
½ cup chopped pecans or walnuts
¾ cup brown sugar
¼ cup butter, melted
¾ cup boiling water

Mix together the flour, sugar, baking powder, cinnamon, salt, and cloves. Add milk and beat until smooth. Stir in pears and nuts. Turn into an ungreased 2-quart casserole dish.

In a separate bowl, mix together the brown sugar, melted butter, and boiling water. Pour evenly over the batter.

Bake at 375° for 45 minutes.

Notes:

Notes:

Pecan Pie

3 eggs
1 cup corn syrup
¾ cup sugar
2 T. butter, melted
1 tsp. salt
1 cup chopped pecans
1 unbaked pie crust

In a medium mixing bowl, beat eggs well. Add corn syrup, sugar, melted butter, and salt and mix well.

Place pecans in the bottom of unbaked pie shell. Pour egg mixture over pecans.

Bake at 350° for 50-60 minutes or until a knife inserted comes out clean.

Popcorn Balls

5 quarts popped corn
2 cups sugar
1½ cups water
½ tsp. salt
½ cup light Karo syrup
1 tsp. vinegar
1 tsp. vanilla

Keep popcorn warm and crisp in a large roasting pan in oven turned to 300° while preparing syrup.

Grease sides and bottom of a large saucepan and add the sugar, water, salt, Karo syrup, and vinegar. Cook until candy thermometer reaches 250°. Remove from heat and add the vanilla.

Slowly pour the syrup evenly over the popped corn, mixing well with a large buttered spoon to coat. Butter your hands and press into approximately 25 balls, being careful not to burn your hands as you work.

Popcorn Birthday Cake

12 cups popped corn (unsalted)
1 12-ounce package peanuts, no paper skins
6 T. butter
1 10.5-oz. bag marshmallows
1 tsp. vanilla
½ tsp. salt
1 12-oz. package mini M&Ms

Generously butter a tube (bundt) pan and set aside. Place the popcorn and peanuts in a very large mixing bowl.

In a saucepan over low heat, melt the butter and marshmallows together, stirring constantly so the mixture doesn't burn. Add the vanilla and salt and stir to blend. Immediately pour the mixture over the popcorn. Butter your hands and mix with your hands quickly. Add the M&Ms and finish mixing, still using your hands. Press firmly into the prepared cake pan and let stand for at least 1 hour.

When ready to serve, unmold the cake onto a serving plate and add candles.

Notes:

Notes:

Pumpkin Coconut Pudding Dessert

1 cup flour
1 cup shredded coconut
½ cup shortening

Crust

Mix the first three ingredients together thoroughly and press into the bottom of a 9 x 13-inch baking pan. Bake at 350° for 10 minutes.

Pudding

1 quart canned pumpkin
1½ cups sugar
4 eggs
½ cup milk
1 tsp. vanilla
2 tsp. cinnamon

While the crust is baking mix together the canned pumpkin, sugar, eggs, milk, vanilla, and cinnamon for the pudding, in the order given. Pour over the crust and continue baking at 350° for another 40-50 minutes.

Quick Leftover Rice Pudding

1 large package vanilla instant pudding mix
2 cups cold milk
1 cup cooked rice

In a bowl, combine pudding mix and milk; beat for 1-2 minutes until well blended. Stir in the rice. Chill well.

Revel Bars

1 cup butter

2 cups brown sugar

2 eggs

2 tsp. vanilla

2½ cups flour

1 tsp. baking soda

½ tsp. salt

3 cups oatmeal

1 T. butter (for filling)

2 cans sweetened condensed milk

2 cups chocolate chips or butterscotch chips

1 cup chopped nuts

In an electric mixer, beat the butter until smooth. Add the brown sugar and blend thoroughly. Next beat in the eggs and vanilla.

In another bowl, stir together the flour, baking soda, and salt. Add the oatmeal and stir again. Gradually stir the flour mixture into the butter and brown sugar mixture. Set aside for now.

In a medium saucepan, combine the 1 T. butter, sweetened condensed milk, and chocolate (or butterscotch) chips. Over low heat, cook until the chips melt, stirring often. Remove from heat and stir in the nuts.

Press ⅔ of the oatmeal mixture into the bottom of an ungreased 15 x 10-inch baking pan. Spread chocolate mixture over the top. Using a spoon and your fingers, dot the remaining oatmeal mixture over the chocolate.

Bake in a 350° oven about 25 minutes or until top is lightly brown. Chocolate mixture will still look a bit moist. Cool and then cut into bars or squares.

Notes:

DESSERTS

Notes:

Rhubarb Chess Pie

2 cups rhubarb, cut into small cubes
1 unbaked pie shell
1¼ cups sugar
4 T. butter, softened
3 eggs
1 T. cider vinegar
1 tsp. vanilla
red food coloring (optional)
cinnamon

Place rhubarb in the pie shell.

In a medium bowl, cream together the sugar and butter.

In a small bowl, beat the eggs slightly and then add the vinegar and vanilla. Add to the sugar mixture and mix well. Tint with a bit of red food coloring, if desired. Pour over the rhubarb and sprinkle cinnamon over the top.

Bake at 350° for 50-60 minutes or until the pie is puffed and golden.

Rhubarb Coffee Cake

1½ cups sugar
½ cup butter
1 egg, beaten
2 cups flour
½ tsp. salt
1 tsp. baking soda
1 cup sour milk or buttermilk
2 cups rhubarb, chopped
1 tsp. vanilla
cinnamon sugar

Cream together sugar and butter. Beat in egg. Sift together dry ingredients and add alternately with the sour milk. Gently stir in rhubarb and vanilla. Spread in a lightly greased 9 x 13-inch baking dish and sprinkle with cinnamon sugar. Bake at 350° for 45-50 minutes or until done.

Rhubarb Custard Pie

3 cups fresh rhubarb, diced
1 unbaked pie shell
½ cup sugar
2 T. cornstarch
¼ tsp. salt
1 egg
¾ cup light Karo syrup
1 T. butter, softened

Place the rhubarb into the pie shell.

In a bowl, combine the sugar, cornstarch, and salt. Add the egg and beat well. Add the corn syrup and butter and beat well again. Pour over the rhubarb.

Bake for 15 minutes at 450° and then reduce heat to 350° and bake for 30 minutes more.

Rice Pudding

1½ cups water
¾ cup uncooked white rice
2 cups milk, divided
⅓ cup sugar
¼ tsp. salt
1 egg, beaten
⅔ cup raisins (optional)
1 T. butter
½ tsp. vanilla

In a medium saucepan, bring 1½ cups water to a boil. Add rice and stir. Cover, reduce heat, and simmer for 20 minutes.

When the rice is cooked, in another saucepan add the cooked rice, 1½ cups milk, sugar, and salt. Cook over medium heat until thick and creamy, about 15 to 20 minutes. Stir in remaining ½ cup milk, the beaten egg, and the raisins, if using them. Cook over low heat 2 minutes more, stirring constantly.

Remove from heat and stir in the butter and vanilla.

Notes:

> You can preach a better sermon with your life than with your lips.

Rocky Road Fudge

2 6-oz. packages chocolate chips
2 T. butter
1 can sweetened condensed milk
1½ tsp. vanilla
½ cup chopped nuts
1 10.5-oz. package miniature marshmallows

In a heavy saucepan over low heat, melt together the chocolate chips, butter, and sweetened condensed milk. Remove from heat and stir in vanilla and chopped nuts.

Place the miniature marshmallows in a large bowl. Pour chocolate mixture over the marshmallows and mix thoroughly.

Spread into a waxed-paper-lined 13 x 9-inch pan. Chill at least 2 hours. Turn fudge out onto a cutting board, peel off the paper, and cut into squares.

Seven-Layer Cookies

½ cup butter, melted
1½ cups graham cracker crumbs
1 cup chopped nuts
1 6-oz. package chocolate chips
1 6-oz. package butterscotch chips
1⅓ cups coconut
1 can condensed milk

Pour melted butter into a 9 x 13-inch baking pan. Sprinkle in order given: graham cracker crumbs, nuts, chocolate chips, butterscotch chips, and coconut. Drizzle the condensed milk over all.

Bake at 325° for 20 minutes or until lightly browned. Cool in pan for 15 minutes before cutting into squares.

Shoo-Fly Pie

1 cup molasses
½ cup brown sugar
2 eggs, beaten
1 cup hot water
1 tsp. baking soda, dissolved in hot water
2 8-inch unbaked pie crusts
2 cups flour
¾ cup brown sugar
⅓ cup butter
½ tsp. cinnamon

Mix the first five ingredients thoroughly together to make a syrup. Divide mixture in half and pour into the two unbaked pie shells. Thoroughly mix together the rest of the ingredients for a crumb topping. Divide and sprinkle crumb topping onto the two pies.

Bake at 450° for 10 minutes and then reduce heat to 350° and continue baking until done, about another 30 minutes.

Snickerdoodles

1 cup butter, softened (do not use margarine)
2 cups sugar
2 eggs
¼ cup milk
1 tsp. vanilla
3¾ cups flour
¾ tsp. baking powder
cinnamon sugar

Cream together the butter and sugar; add to this mixture the eggs, milk, and vanilla, one at a time, beating well after each addition. Sift together the flour and baking powder and add the creamed mixture.

Roll dough into little balls and then roll in a mixture of sugar and cinnamon. Place on an ungreased cookie sheet and flatten slightly.

Bake at 375° for 10-12 minutes.

Notes:

Strawberry Pie

1 quart strawberries, washed, drained, and hulled
1 cup sugar
3 T. cornstarch
½ cup cream cheese, softened
1 baked and cooled pie crust

Save out 2 cups of the choicest berries.

Mash remaining berries until juice is extracted. If necessary, add water in order to make 1½ cups liquid, using all parts of berries (this will be thick and lumpy with mashed berries).

In another bowl, mix together the sugar and cornstarch.

In a large saucepan, bring the berry juice to boiling, gradually stirring in the sugar and cornstarch mixture. Cook over medium-low heat, stirring constantly, until boiling. Boil 1 minute, continuing to stir constantly. Cool.

Spread the softened cream cheese over the bottom of the cooled, baked pie shell, being careful not to pull up the crust from the bottom of the pan (use your fingers, if necessary). Spread the saved berries over the top of the cream cheese in the pie shell. Pour the thickened juice mixture over the berries, evenly distributing the syrup.

Chill at least 2 hours. Top with sweetened whipped cream right before serving.

Strawberry Tapioca Pudding

2 cups strawberries, washed and hulled
1 cup sugar, divided
3 cups boiling water
½ cup quick-cooking tapioca
¼ tsp. salt
2 tsp. butter
1 tsp. lemon juice
¼ tsp. vanilla
red food coloring (optional)

Mash strawberries with ½ cup of the sugar and set aside.

In a large saucepan, combine the boiling water, tapioca, and salt; let stand for 10 minutes. Turn to medium heat and cook for about 15 minutes or until the tapioca is clear.

Remove from heat and immediately stir in butter and remaining sugar. Whisk in lemon juice and vanilla. (You can add a few drops of red food coloring at this point if you want pink color throughout.) Stir in strawberries, mixing well. Chill for several hours and then serve topped with whipped cream.

Super Easy Chocolate Cake

2 cups sugar
2 cups flour
½ tsp. salt
2 tsp. baking powder
2 T. (slightly heaping) baking cocoa
1½ cups milk
2 T. butter, melted
2 eggs

In a large bowl, with a large spoon or spatula, mix together the dry ingredients. Add the milk, butter, and eggs and mix well. Pour into a greased 8-inch square baking pan and bake at 350° for 45 minutes or until done.

Serve with powdered sugar sprinkled on top.

If you are feeding a lot of people, simply double all of the ingredients and bake in a larger pan.

Notes:

Sweet Zucchini Bread

3 cups flour
1 tsp. baking soda
¼ tsp. baking powder
1 tsp. salt
3 tsp. cinnamon
½ cup nuts, chopped
3 eggs, beaten
1 cup oil
2 cups sugar
2 cups zucchini, grated
2 tsp. vanilla

In a large mixing bowl, mix together the flour, baking soda, baking powder, salt, cinnamon, and nuts. Then add the rest of the ingredients and mix until the batter is well blended.

Divide the batter into 2 greased loaf pans and bake at 325° for 1 hour or until done. Remove from pans at once and cool on a baking rack.

Tapioca Fluff

6 cups milk
6 T. quick-cooking tapioca
1½ cups sugar, divided
4 eggs, separated

Heat together the milk, quick-cooking tapioca, 1 cup sugar, and 4 egg yolks, stirring constantly. Bring to a boil and cook for 5 minutes.

Remove from heat and beat the 4 egg whites with the remaining sugar until you have stiff peaks. Gently add to the tapioca mixture and stir together for 2 minutes; pour into 12 dessert bowls.

Vanilla Cornstarch Pudding

⅓ cup sugar
¼ cup cornstarch
¼ tsp. salt
2¾ cups milk
2 T. butter
1 tsp. vanilla

In a medium saucepan, mix together the sugar, cornstarch, and salt. Gradually stir in milk, stirring constantly, to blend. Bring the mixture to a boil over medium heat, stirring constantly. Boil for 1 minute. Remove from heat and add the butter and vanilla.

Whoopie Pies

½ cup shortening
1 cup brown sugar, packed
1 egg
2 cups flour
¼ cup cocoa
1 tsp. baking powder
1 tsp. baking soda
1 tsp. salt
1 cup milk
1 tsp. vanilla
Whoopie Pie Filling (recipe follows)

In a large mixing bowl, cream together the shortening, sugar, and egg.

In another bowl, combine the flour, cocoa, baking powder, baking soda, and salt.

In another small bowl, stir together the milk and vanilla.

Add the dry ingredients and the milk mixture to the creamed shortening mixture, alternating between the two. Beat until smooth.

Drop batter onto greased cookie sheets (you'll make about 18

Notes:

A man who gives his children habits of industry provides for them better than by giving them a fortune.

Notes:

He that rises late must trot all day and shall scarce overtake his business at night.

cookies; you'll need an even number of cookies because you use two cookies for each Whoopie Pie). Spread the batter so it's in a circle and is flat; the cookies will be about 4 inches across. Bake at 350° for 15 minutes or until the cookies are firm to the touch. Cool completely on a wire rack.

Make Whoopie Pie Filling (recipe below). When the cookies are completely cool, spread the flat side (bottom) of one with a generous amount of filling. Top with another cookie, pressing down gently to distribute the filling evenly. Repeat with all the cookies. Wrap Whoopie Pies individually in plastic wrap because they tend to stick together and store them in a single layer.

Whoopie Pie Filling

1 cup shortening
1½ cups powdered sugar
2 cups marshmallow cream
1½ tsp. vanilla

In a medium bowl, beat together the shortening, sugar, and marshmallow cream. Stir in vanilla until well blended.

MIXES AND MISCELLANEOUS

Amish housewives are a busy bunch, and when there is a way to make work lighter or go more quickly—and that doesn't go against the *ordnung*—they will take advantage of these time-savers.

In this section, among lots of other miscellany, you will find mix-ahead recipes you can whip up in large batches that can be used when you need a quick menu item to round out a meal. The Amish are also known for their frugality, and many of these mixes can be made for much less than it would cost to buy the same items from a store already prepared and boxed.

If there is any consolation in Christ, if any comfort of love, if any fellowship of the Spirit, if any affection and mercy, fulfill my joy by being like-minded, having the same love, being of one accord, of one mind. Let nothing be done through selfish ambition or conceit, but in lowliness of mind let each esteem others better than himself. Let each of you look out not only for his own interests, but also for the interests of others.

PHILIPPIANS 2:1-4

Oh, Lord, You are good; Your mercy endures forever. I pray You will look with favor upon my family. Help them to see the benefit of being called Your chosen ones. May they rejoice in gladness and glory in their inheritance, which is Christ the King. We give You thanks, Lord, and praise Your holy name.

Amish Church Peanut Butter Spread

3 lb. peanut butter, crunchy or creamy

2 quarts light Karo syrup

2 quarts marshmallow cream

Mix together until smooth. Can add a bit more Karo syrup if it's too thick. This spread is good on bananas, toast, and spooned over ice cream.

Amish Church Peanut Butter Spread (Small Batch)

1 cup light Karo syrup

½ cup peanut butter

¼ cup marshmallow cream

Mix together all ingredients. Store in an airtight container. If you keep it in the refrigerator, let it sit at room temperature before spreading it on sandwiches.

Barbecue Sauce

½ cup catsup

1 T. vinegar

1 T. sugar

1 T. prepared mustard

1 T. Worcestershire sauce

Mix all ingredients together. Use to baste chicken or beef, either on the barbecue or in the oven.

Notes:

Barbecue Sauce for Chicken

¼ cup vinegar
¼ cup catsup
2 T. oil
2 T. soy sauce
1 T. Worcestershire sauce
1 tsp. dry mustard
1 tsp. salt

Mix all ingredients together in a saucepan and, stirring often, bring to a boil. Cool and either use immediately or keep in the refrigerator until ready to use.

Better Butter

1 lb. butter
1¼ cups canola oil

Bring butter to room temperature. Combine butter and oil in a blender or with an electric mixer and blend until smooth. Pour into containers and store in the refrigerator.

Bird Suet That Won't Go Rancid

1 cup crunchy peanut butter
1 cup lard, room temperature
2 cups quick-cooking oats
2 cups cornmeal
1 cup flour
⅓ cup sugar
Leftover nuts of any kind, chopped small

In a saucepan, melt the peanut butter and lard together over medium-low heat. Stir in the remaining ingredients and pour into an 8 x 8-inch pan. Cool completely and cut into squares that will fit in a suet cage. Wrap unused squares in plastic wrap and store in a cool, dry place until needed.

The Amish love to feed and watch birds. It's quite common to see an Amish farmhouse with numerous bird houses perched high atop posts at the edge of their yards and gardens.

Brined-in-the-Jar Dill Pickles

Per Jar
Cucumbers
4-6 cloves garlic
½ hot chili pepper (use a whole one if you like it spicy)
1 tsp. pickling spice
3-4 sprigs fresh dill plus ½ tsp. dill weed
2 T. salt
1 cup vinegar, hot but not boiling
boiling water to fill jar

Wash and cut off the ends of small pickling cucumbers. If using larger cukes, halve or quarter lengthwise. Then pack each jar with cucumbers, garlic, chili pepper, pickling spice, dill, and salt. Add vinegar and boiling water to fill. Leave no headspace.

Immediately seal with clean rings and seals that have been kept in simmering water. Adjust caps and shake each jar. Invert on a towel until cool. Shake jars every day. Your pickles will be ready to eat in 2 weeks.

Notes:

You make 1 quart jar at a time. Multiply ingredients by how many jars of pickles you wish to prepare.

Catsup

2½ gallons tomato juice
½ cup salt
2 medium onions, shredded
1 tsp. cinnamon
1 tsp. ground cloves
2½ cups vinegar
8 cups sugar
½ cup flour

In a large pot, boil down a third of the tomato juice; add salt, onions, cinnamon, cloves, and vinegar. Mix well. Add sugar and flour to juice, stirring constantly. Bring to a boil and simmer until ready to can. Fill pints jars and consult a canning guide for processing directions.

Notes:

Chicken-Flavored Rice Mix

4 cups uncooked long-grain white rice

4 T. instant chicken bouillon

1 tsp. salt

2 tsp. dried tarragon

2 tsp. dried parsley flakes

¼ tsp. pepper

Combine all ingredients and blend very well. Put 1⅓ cups rice mix into 3 1-pint airtight containers. Store in a cool, dry place. Date the container and use within 8 months.

To Use

1⅓ cups Chicken-Flavored Rice Mix

2¼ cups cold water

1 T. butter

Place the ingredients in a saucepan and bring to a boil. Then cover, reduce heat, and cook for 20 minutes or until liquid is absorbed and rice is done.

Chow Chow

1 cup green tomatoes, chopped

1 cup bell peppers, chopped

1 cup cabbage, chopped

1 whole cucumber, chopped

1 cup onions, chopped

2 quarts water

¼ cup salt

1 cup carrots, chopped

1 cup green beans, chopped

2 tsp. mustard seed

2 tsp. celery seed

2 cups vinegar

2 cups sugar

Soak tomatoes, peppers, cabbage, cucumber, and onions

Try adding cauliflower and celery to your Chow Chow if you like those vegetables.

overnight in water and salt. Drain. Cook carrots and green beans for 10 minutes and drain. Mix all ingredients. Heat to a boil. Pack in jars and seal. (Follow safe canning instructions from the *Ball Blue Book* or other up-to-date canning guide.)

Frozen Strawberry Jam

4 cups sugar

1 quart strawberries, washed, hulled, and crushed (makes 2 cups crushed)

1 box fruit pectin

¾ cup water

Place the crushed strawberries and sugar in a large bowl. Mix well and set aside for 10 minutes, stirring occasionally.

In a saucepan, stir the fruit pectin and water together and bring to a boil over high heat, stirring constantly. Boil and stir for 1 minute, and then remove from heat and stir into the strawberry mixture. Stir constantly until the sugar is completely dissolved; this could take several minutes.

Pour jam into clean glass or plastic freezer containers, leaving at least ½-inch headspace. Cover and let stand at room temperature for 24 hours before refrigerating or freezing until ready to use. When using frozen jam, allow to thaw in the refrigerator before using.

Fruit Drops

½ cup sugar

¼ cup plus 2 tsp. Clear Jel

1⅓ cup fruit juice or puree

1 T. lemon juice

Mix together the sugar and Clear Jel. Add Clear Jel mixture to fruit juice or puree in a heavy pot. Cook using medium heat until mixture thickens and comes to a boil, stirring constantly. Add lemon juice; boil 1 minute.

Drop small amounts onto waxed paper and allow to set completely.

Notes:

FLOURS

Most often, cooks use all-purpose flour, but there are other kinds, and they all have their uses:

All-purpose flour. This is the mainstay of a cook's kitchen. It comes either bleached or unbleached and is comprised of wheat from various regions. It's like McDonald's French fries—no matter where you live, the flour will yield predictable results.

Bread flour. Bread flour is a very high protein flour that has a higher gluten content, which is a necessary component in baking light, moist bread. You can buy gluten separately and add a small amount to your bread dough if you experience poor results from your standard flour.

Cake flour. This is the lowest protein flour generally available, and it has been ground

Homemade Baking Powder

2 tsp. cornstarch or arrowroot
2 tsp. cream of tartar
1 tsp. baking soda

Mix together and store in an airtight container.

Large batch baking powder: Mix together one part cornstarch, one part cream of tartar, and one-half part baking soda.

Homemade Grape Juice

firm, ripe grapes
sugar
boiling water

Wash and sterilize quart-size canning jars and lids. Keep warm.

Wash and stem the grapes. Put 1 cup grapes into a hot quart jar. Add ¼ cup sugar per jar and slowly fill with boiling water, leaving ¼-inch headspace. Remove air bubbles, adjust caps, and process 15 minutes in a boiling water bath.

Store in a cool, dark place. Serve well chilled.

Hot Chocolate Mix I

10⅔ cups instant nonfat dry milk
1 6-oz. jar powdered nondairy creamer
2 cups powdered sugar
1 16-oz. can instant chocolate drink mix

Combine all ingredients and mix well. Place in an airtight container or large plastic storage bags. Store in a cool, dry place. Date the container and use within 6 months.

To Use

Add 3 T. Hot Chocolate Mix to 1 cup hot water. Stir to dissolve.

Hot Chocolate Mix II

6½ cups instant nonfat dry milk
1 cup powdered sugar
1 cup granulated sugar
1 cup unsweetened baking cocoa
dash of salt

Combine all ingredients and mix well. Place in an airtight container or large plastic storage bags. Store in a cool, dry place. Date the container and use within 6 months.

To Use

3 T. Hot Chocolate Mix
1 cup hot water or milk

Add the Hot Chocolate Mix to hot water or milk and stir to dissolve.

Lemonade Concentrate

3 T. lemon zest
4 cups sugar
4 cups water
2 cinnamon sticks
Juice of 6 lemons, strained to remove pulp and seeds

In a deep saucepan, combine the lemon zest, sugar, water, and cinnamon sticks. Bring the mixture to a rolling boil. Reduce heat and boil gently, uncovered, for 5 minutes. Remove from heat and cool. Strain the mixture through cheesecloth or a very fine wire sieve. Add the lemon juice to the sugar syrup. Transfer to a glass container that has been cleaned and boiled and refrigerate until needed.

To Make Lemonade

Mix 4 T. lemon syrup with 1 cup of cold water. Fill 2 glasses with ice and pour in the lemonade. Stir and serve.

Notes:

continued

fine and bleached and chlorinated to make it slightly acidic. The resulting flour produces fine-textured, moist cakes and is good to use when making pastry, baking powder biscuits, and cookies.

Notes:

Sometimes God calms the storm, but sometimes He lets the storm rage and calms His child.

Master Biscuit Mix

8½ cups flour
3 T. baking powder
1 T. salt
2 tsp. cream of tartar
1 tsp. baking soda
1½ cups instant nonfat dry milk
2¼ cups shortening

In a large mixing bowl, sift together all dry ingredients. Blend well. With a pastry blender, cut in shortening until evenly distributed and the consistency of coarse cornmeal. Place in an airtight container or large plastic storage bags. Store in a cool, dry place. Date the container and use within 3 months.

This Master Biscuit Mix can be used in place of Bisquick in many recipes, but here are a few recipes to get you started.

Drop Biscuits

3 cups Master Biscuit Mix
¾ cup milk or water

Grease a cookie sheet and set aside. Mix together the Master Biscuit Mix and water or milk. Stir just until blended. Drop dough by tablespoonfuls onto greased cookie sheet. Bake at 450° for 8-10 minutes.

Cheese Biscuits

Make as above but add ⅓ cup shredded Cheddar cheese, 2 T. finely minced fresh onion, and seasonings to taste. You can also fry several pieces of bacon until crisp. Crumble cooked bacon into the cheese dough, mix, and bake.

Rolled Biscuits

3 cups Master Biscuit Mix
⅔ cup milk or water

Mix together the Master Biscuit Mix and water or milk. Cover and let dough stand for 5 minutes. Turn out onto a lightly floured surface and knead about 15 times. Roll out dough to 1½-inch thickness and cut with a floured cutter. Place about 2 inches apart on an ungreased cookie sheet and bake at 450° for 10-12 minutes.

Pancakes or Waffles

2¼ cups Master Biscuit Mix
1 T. sugar
1 egg, beaten
1½ cups milk or water

Combine Master Biscuit Mix and sugar in a mixing bowl and mix well. In a separate bowl, combine egg and milk or water; add all at once to the dry ingredients. Blend well. Let stand for 5-10 minutes and then cook pancakes in a small amount of oil, turning to cook both sides.

Quick Pizza Crust

3¼ cups Master Biscuit Mix
2¼ tsp. (1 package) active dry yeast
½ tsp. salt
¾ cup warm water

Mix together dry ingredients; add warm water and turn out dough on a lightly floured surface. Let stand 5 minutes. Knead dough about 20 times and then pat dough into pizza pan. Top with your favorite pizza sauce and toppings and bake at 425° for 20 minutes or until done.

Super Easy Doughnuts

2 cups Master Biscuit Mix
¼ cup sugar
¼ tsp. cinnamon
¼ tsp. nutmeg
1 tsp. vanilla
1 egg, well beaten
⅓ cup water or milk
Vanilla Glaze (recipe follows)

In a medium bowl, combine Master Biscuit Mix, sugar, cinnamon, and nutmeg. Blend well.

In a small bowl, mix together vanilla, beaten egg, and water or milk. Add all at once to the dry ingredients and stir until well blended. Turn out dough onto a lightly floured surface and knead for at least 5 minutes. Roll out dough to ½-inch thickness and cut with a floured doughnut cutter. Fry in a deep-fat fryer

Notes:

MIXES AND MISCELLANEOUS

Notes:

set to 375° about 1 minute each side or until golden brown. Drain on paper towels and cool slightly. Dip warm doughnuts in Vanilla Glaze.

Vanilla Glaze

1¼ cups powdered sugar
2 T. milk
½ tsp. vanilla

Mix ingredients together in a bowl.

Master Brownie Mix

6 cups flour
4 tsp. baking powder
4 tsp. salt
8 cups sugar
1 8-oz. can unsweetened baking cocoa
2 cups shortening

In a large bowl, sift together the flour, baking powder, and salt. Add the sugar and cocoa and mix again. Add the shortening and work with a pastry cutter until shortening has been well incorporated and the mixture resembles coarse cornmeal. Place in an airtight container or large plastic storage bags. Store in a cool, dry place. Date the container and use within 3 months.

Brownies

2 eggs, beaten
1 tsp. vanilla
2½ cups Master Brownie Mix
½ cup chopped nuts
powdered sugar

Grease and flour an 8 x 8-inch baking dish. In a medium bowl, combine the eggs, vanilla, and Master Brownie Mix. Beat until smooth. Stir in nuts. Pour into prepared pan and bake at 350° for 30-35 minutes. Cool before cutting. Sprinkle top with powdered sugar when ready to serve.

Chewy Chocolate Cookies

2 eggs, beaten
½ cup water
2¼ cups Master Brownie Mix
½ tsp. baking soda
¾ cup flour
1 tsp. vanilla
walnut or pecan halves

Combine eggs and water in a medium bowl. Beat with a fork until well blended. Stir in the Master Brownie Mix, baking soda, flour, and vanilla. Blend well. Drop by teaspoonfuls onto greased cookie sheets about 2 inches apart. Lightly push a walnut or pecan half into the top of each cookie. Bake at 375° for 10-12 minutes. Cool on wire racks.

Variation: Roll dough balls into powdered sugar before baking.

Master Cornbread Mix

4 cups flour
1½ cups instant nonfat dry milk
1 T. salt
¾ cup sugar
¼ cup baking powder
1 cup shortening
4½ cups cornmeal

In a large mixing bowl, combine the flour, dry milk, salt, sugar, and baking powder and mix well. Add the shortening and work with a pastry cutter until shortening has been well incorporated and the mixture resembles coarse cornmeal. Add the cornmeal and mix well again. Place in airtight container or large plastic storage bags. Store in a cool, dry place. Date the container and use within 3 months.

Notes:

You can also add cooked, crumbled bacon, shredded Cheddar cheese, onions, and herbs to your corn muffins or cornbread for a tasty alternative.

Notes:

Corn Muffins

1 egg, beaten
1¼ cups water
2¾ cups Master Cornbread Mix

Combine egg and water in a small bowl. In a medium bowl measure out the Master Cornbread Mix; add egg and water mixture all at once to the Master Cornbread Mix and stir just until blended. Fill buttered muffin tins ⅔ full and bake at 425° for 15-20 minutes or until golden brown.

Cornbread

Follow the recipe for Corn Muffins but pour the batter into a buttered 8 x 8-inch baking dish. Bake at 400° for 25-30 minutes or until golden brown. Serve with honey butter.

Honey Butter

1 cup butter, softened
1¼ cups honey

Blend together the butter and honey using an electric mixer until light and fluffy, about 5 minutes. Store in refrigerator.

Master Oatmeal Muffin Mix

3 cups flour
1 cup instant nonfat dry milk
3½ tsp. baking powder
1½ tsp. salt
½ cup sugar
1 cup brown sugar
1½ cups shortening
3 cups rolled oats

In a large mixing bowl, sift together the flour, dry milk, baking powder, salt, and sugar. Mix well; add the brown sugar and mix well again. Add the shortening and work with a pastry cutter until shortening has been well incorporated and the mixture resembles coarse cornmeal. Stir in oats and mix well. Place in an airtight container or large plastic storage bags. Store in a cool, dry place. Date the container and use within 3 months.

Oatmeal Muffins

3 cups Master Oatmeal Muffin Mix
1 egg
⅔ cup water or milk

Put Master Oatmeal Muffin Mix in a medium size mixing bowl. Combine the egg and water or milk and pour all at once into the dry ingredients. Stir just until moistened; the batter will be lumpy. Fill buttered muffin tins ⅔ full and bake at 400° for 15-20 minutes or until golden brown.

Master Pancake Mix

10 cups flour
2½ cups instant nonfat dry milk
½ cup sugar
¼ cup baking powder
2 T. salt

Combine all ingredients in a large bowl and mix well. Place in an airtight container or large plastic storage bags. Store in a cool, dry place. Date the container and use within 8 months.

Basic Pancakes

1½ cups Master Pancake Mix
1 egg, beaten
1 cup water
3 T. oil

Put Master Pancake Mix in a medium mixing bowl. Combine egg, water, and oil and mix into the dry ingredients. Add more water for thinner pancakes. Blend well. Let stand 5 minutes and then cook pancakes, turning once, until golden on both sides.

Notes:

Oven Puff Pancakes

4 T. butter, divided
⅔ cup Pancake Mix
4 eggs
⅔ cup milk

Preheat oven to 450°. Divide butter between two 9-inch pie plates and place in the oven to melt the butter. Meanwhile, in a blender, combine the rest of the ingredients and mix well. Pour batter in the two pie plates and return to the oven. Bake about 18 minutes or until pancakes have puffed up and are golden brown. Do not open oven door while the pancakes are baking or they will fall. You can serve these with butter and syrup or a fresh fruit topping and a dollop of sour cream.

Mexican Rice Mix

4 cups uncooked long-grain white rice
½ cup green pepper flakes or dehydrated green pepper
4 tsp. salt
5 tsp. parsley flakes
1 tsp. dried basil

Combine all ingredients. Stir until very well blended. Put 1½ cups rice mix into three 1-pint airtight containers. Store in a cool, dry place. Date the container and use within 8 months.

To Use

1½ cups Mexican Rice Mix
2½ cups cold water
1 T. butter or oil

Combine all ingredients together in a saucepan and bring to a boil. Cover and reduce heat and cook for 20 minutes or until all the liquid is absorbed and rice is done.

Orange Float Mix

4 cups instant nonfat dry milk
2 cups powdered orange drink mix (such as Tang)
1 cup sugar

Combine all ingredients and mix well. Place in an airtight container or large plastic storage bags. Store in a cool, dry place. Date the container and use within 6 months.

To Use

½ cup Orange Float Mix
1 cup water
2 ice cubes

Mix together all ingredients in a blender and serve immediately.

Variations: You can add frozen or fresh fruit or berries, flavored or plain yogurt, or anything that suits your taste.

Onion Dip Mix

1 T. instant minced onion
1 T. grated Parmesan cheese
1½ tsp. instant beef bouillon
¼ tsp. garlic salt

Combine all ingredients and mix well. Place mix onto a 6-inch square of aluminum foil and fold in edges to seal airtight. You can make a number of these packets at one time; place all the packets in a large storage container or bag. Date the container and use within 4 months.

To Use

1 packet Onion Dip Mix
1 cup sour cream

Mix together Onion Dip Mix and sour cream. Chill well before serving.

Variations: Substitute 1 cup cottage cheese or 1 8-oz. package of cream cheese for the sour cream.

Notes:

When an Amish couple gets ready to retire and hand over their farm—usually to the youngest son and his wife—they will stay on the farm in a *Dawdy* house. *Dawdy* houses are often attached to the main house, with a separate entrance and kitchen. Older homes might have 2 *Dawdy* houses, where grandparents and great-grandparents live alongside the young couple.

Onion-Flavored Rice Mix

4 cups uncooked long-grain white rice
2 packages dry onion soup mix
1 T. parsley flakes
1 tsp. salt

Combine ingredients in a large bowl. Mix very well. Put 1⅓ cups rice mix into three 1-pint airtight containers. Store in a cool, dry place. Date the container and use within 8 months.

To Use

1⅓ cups Onion-Flavored Rice Mix
2¼ cups water
1 T. butter

Combine all the ingredients in a saucepan and bring to a boil. Cover, reduce heat, and cook for 20 minutes or until liquid is absorbed and rice is done.

Playdough

1 cup white flour
¼ cup salt
2 T. cream of tartar
1 cup water
2 tsp. food coloring
1 T. oil

Mix the flour, salt, and cream of tartar in a medium pot. In a separate bowl, combine the water, food coloring, and oil and add that to the flour mixture and mix together. Cook over medium heat, stirring, for 3-5 minutes. It will look like a globby mess while you are stirring.

When the mixture forms a ball in the center of the pot, turn out onto a lightly floured surface and knead until it looks like Play-Doh. Store in an airtight container or a plastic storage bag.

Ranch-Style Dressing and Dip Mix

For Each Packet

2 tsp. instant minced onion

½ tsp. salt

⅛ tsp. garlic powder

1 T. parsley flakes

2 T. buttermilk powder

Combine all ingredients until very well mixed. For each packet, place the mixed ingredients onto a 6-inch square of aluminum foil and fold to make airtight. You can make a number of these packets at one time; place all the packets in a large storage container or bag. Date the container and use within 6 months.

Dressing

1 packet Ranch-Style Dressing and Dip Mix

1 cup mayonnaise

¾ cup water

Combine all ingredients in a quart jar and shake until well blended. Chill before serving.

Dip

1 packet Ranch-Style Dressing and Dip Mix

1 cup mayonnaise

1 cup sour cream

Combine all ingredients in a quart jar and shake until well blended. Chill before serving.

Notes:

Red Beet Eggs

1 15-oz. can beets; do not drain
1 onion, thinly sliced
12 hard-boiled eggs, shelled and left whole
¼ cup sugar
½ cup vinegar

Drain liquid from the beets and place in a saucepan. Place the beets, onion, and eggs in a large bowl (do not use plastic or metal).

To the beet liquid add the sugar and vinegar and bring the mixture to a boil. Turn down the heat and simmer for 15 minutes. Remove from heat and cool slightly before pouring over the beets, onion, and eggs. Cover the bowl with a lid or plastic wrap and set in the refrigerator for at least a day. Two or three days are better because the longer they sit, the deeper the color of the eggs and onions.

Snitz

Peel and core apples and slice into eighths. Place in a 200° oven and leave the oven door open to let the steam escape. Stir apples often. Drying can take as long as 24 hours.

Store in jars, but not necessarily airtight.

To use the snitz, soak overnight in cold water to soften.

Notes:

An industrious wife is the best savings account.

Spicy and Sweet Barbecue Sauce

1 quart water
2 10-oz. cans tomato paste
2 lemons, seeded and cut into eighths
2 cloves garlic, minced
1 onion, chopped
6 bay leaves
1 tsp. celery salt
1 tsp. allspice
1 tsp. pepper
1½ tsp. ground red pepper or pepper flakes
2 tsp. salt
1½ cups brown sugar, packed
1½ cups cider vinegar

Combine all ingredients in a large stockpot and bring to a boil over medium heat. Reduce heat and simmer, uncovered, for 45 minutes. Remove the lemon slices and bay leaves and discard.

When slightly cooled, transfer the barbecue sauce to sterilized jars with tight-fitting lids and refrigerate. This sauce can keep indefinitely if kept refrigerated.

Vegetable Dip Mix

For Each Packet
1 T. dried chives
½ tsp. dill weed
1 tsp. garlic salt
½ tsp. paprika

Combine all ingredients until well blended. Place the mixture onto a 6-inch square of aluminum foil and fold over to make airtight. Make a number of these packets at one time; place packets in an airtight container or storage bag. Use within 6 months.

Notes:

Notes:

To Use

1 packet Vegetable Dip Mix

1 T. lemon juice

1 cup mayonnaise

1 cup sour cream

Combine all ingredients. Chill well before serving.

White Sauce Mix

2 cups instant nonfat dry milk

1 cup flour

2 tsp. salt

1 cup butter

In a large bowl, combine the dry milk, flour, and salt. Mix well. Add the butter and work with a pastry cutter until the butter has been well incorporated and the mixture resembles coarse cornmeal. Lightly pack in an airtight container or large plastic storage bags. Store in refrigerator. Date the container and use within 2 months.

Basic White Sauce

¼-½ cup White Sauce Mix (depending on how thin you want the finished sauce to be)

1 cup cold water or milk

salt and pepper to taste

In a small saucepan, combine the White Sauce Mix and water or milk. Cook, stirring, over low heat, until smooth and thickened. Season with salt and pepper to taste.

Variations: You can substitute tomato juice or broth for the water. To make a cheese sauce, add ¾ cup shredded Cheddar or Velveeta cheese when mixture thickens and stir until cheese is melted.

> Many Amish in a community have the same first and last names, so in order to distinguish who exactly they are referring to, they make extensive use of nicknames. You might hear names such as "Jake's Suzie," "Chicken Elam," or "Butter Mose."

SUBSTITUTIONS AND MEASUREMENTS

Substitutions

1 tsp. baking powder	⅓ tsp. baking soda plus ½ tsp. cream of tartar or ¼ tsp. baking soda plus ⅓ cup sour milk
1 T. cornstarch	2 T. flour
2 T. tapioca	3 T. flour
2 egg yolks	1 whole egg
1 cup fresh milk	½ cup evaporated milk plus ½ cup water or ⅓ cup dry milk plus 1 cup water
1 cup sour milk	1 cup buttermilk or yogurt or 1⅓ T. vinegar or lemon juice plus milk to make 1 cup
1 cup sour cream	1 cup plain yogurt
1 cup sugar	¾ cup honey, molasses, or corn syrup; reduce liquid in recipe by ¼ cup, add ¼ tsp. baking soda, and reduce oven temperature by 25°.
1 cup brown sugar	Mix together 1 cup white sugar with 2 T. molasses
1 square unsweetened chocolate	3 T. cocoa

Substituting Measurements

3 tsp. = 1 T.

2 T. = ⅛ cup

4 T. = ¼ cup

8 T. = ½ cup

16 T. = 1 cup

5 T. + 1 tsp. = ⅓ cup

12 T. = ¾ cup

4 oz. = ½ cup

8 oz. = 1 cup

16 oz. = 1 lb.

1 oz. = 2 T. fat/liquid

2 cups fat = 1 lb.

2 cups = 1 pint

2 cups sugar = 1 lb.

⅝ cup = ½ cup + 2 T.

⅞ cup = ¾ cup + 2 T.

1 oz. butter = 2 T.

1 lb. butter = 2 cups or 4 sticks

1 pint = 2 cups

2 pints = 1 quart

1 quart = 4 cups

dash = less than 1/8 tsp.

pinch = as much as can be taken between tip of finger and thumb

Approximate Measurements

1 lemon makes 3 T. juice

1 lemon makes 1 tsp. grated peel

1 orange makes ⅓ cup juice

1 orange makes 2 tsp. grated peel

1 medium chopped onion makes ½ cup

1 lb. unshelled walnuts makes 1½-1¾ cups shelled

1 lb. unshelled almonds makes ¾-1 cup shelled

8-10 egg whites make 1 cup

12-14 egg yolks make 1 cup

1 lb. shredded cheese make 4 cups

1 cup unwhipped cream makes 2 cups whipped

4 oz. (1-1¼ cups) uncooked macaroni make 2 cups cooked

7 oz. spaghetti make 4 cups cooked

4 oz. (1½-2 cups) uncooked noodles make 2 cups cooked

Commercial Container Sizes

If you want to substitute your home-canned or frozen foods in recipes that call for commercially canned or frozen foods, use this chart to help determine the quantity needed.

6 oz. = ¾ cup

8 oz. = 1 cup

10½ oz. = 1¼ cups

14½-oz. can evaporated milk = 1⅔ cups

15-oz. can sweetened condensed milk = 1⅓ cups

15½ oz. = 1¾ cups

46 oz. (juices and fruit drinks) = 5¾ cups

10-oz. box of frozen vegetables = 2 cups

20-oz. bag of frozen vegetables = 4 cups

RESOURCES

Lehman's
One Lehman Circle
P.O. Box 270
Kidron, OH 44636
888-438-5346
www.lehmans.com

Lehman's supplies the Amish and others with a wide variety of items for those who live without electricity or prefer a more self-sufficient lifestyle. You can ask for a paper catalog to be sent to your home for a small fee (it's worth the price) or you can go online to browse and shop. Lehman's has about everything you could wish for—lanterns (including a large selection of Aladdin lamps and all replacement parts), nonelectric kitchen appliances and gadgets, canning utensils, barn and farm supplies, wood-burning cookstoves, propane refrigerators, wash day supplies, sewing machines, furniture and toys, garden implements—if you can think of it, they probably have it or have access to a supplier.

The Budget
P.O. Box 249
Sugarcreek, OH 44681
330-852-4634
www.thebudgetnewspaper.com

Known as the "Amish Newspaper," *The Budget* has been around since 1890. The national edition, published weekly, is filled with letters sent in by Amish and Mennonite "scribes" who relay the news of interest from their communities. Because telephones aren't a part of everyday life for many Amish families, *The Budget* is a handy way to keep abreast of events in surrounding, and sometimes far-flung, communities where they often have extended family. Even if you're not Amish or Mennonite, *The Budget* is good reading.

Chupp's Herbs & Fabrics
27539 Londick Road
Burr Oak, MI 49030
269-659-3950

Chupp's sells dietary supplements, shoes, fabrics, Mutza suits, hats and gloves, toys and games, wagons, hand-powered small kitchen appliances, and much more.

You can call or write for a free catalog. More than 100 pages are jam-packed with products and testimonials, many from satisfied Amish customers. Makes for interesting reading.

Gohn Brothers
P.O. Box 1110
105 S. Main Street
Middlebury, IN 46540
800-595-0031
www.gohnbrothers.com

Gohn Brothers has been around for more than 100 years and sells Amish and Plain clothing and footwear (including old-fashioned high-topped shoes), books and games, sewing and quilting fabric, needles and accessories, and black Amish bonnets. You can call or write and ask for their free catalog.

Anabaptist Bookstore

875 N. Pacific Hwy.
Woodburn, OR 97071
www.anabaptistbooks.com

This bookstore has an excellent website that carries many resources from Amish and Conservative Mennonite publishers—many of whom do not have a web presence. There are books on family and marriage, victorious living, youth and adult fiction, Bibles and study aids, and the complete education curriculum from Rod and Staff and Christian Light publishers. There are also a cappella music tapes and CDs for sale featuring Mennonite quartets, quintets, and choirs.

Ball Corporation

www.freshpreserving.com

Every few years, the Ball Corporation puts out a new edition of their *Blue Book,* which is one of the best resources for home preserving, whether you want to can, freeze, or dehydrate your foods. This handy book is also chock-full of excellent recipes and ideas. If you only ever have one book on preserving, this is the one to get. An added bonus is that the book is quite inexpensive. The 100th Anniversary edition (1909–2009) sells for $6.99 at my local store. No kitchen should be without a copy—it's just that good.

Mennonite Relief Sales

Mennonite Central Committee
704 Main Street
P.O. Box 500
Akron, PA 17501

You can contact the MCC for a current listing of Mennonite Relief Sales that are held annually in most states and Canadian provinces.

While this is not specifically Amish, the Mennonite Relief Sales are so much fun to attend that it's worth going to at least once if there is one near your area. The sales are organized locally by volunteers from Mennonite and Brethren in Christ churches, so each location has its own flavor. Begun in the 1950s, the Relief Sales are designed to raise money to help the less fortunate throughout the world.

You will find many items for sale, including beautiful handmade quilts, which the Relief Sales are especially known for, as well as furniture, needlework, pottery, woodwork, and paintings. Antiques and other quality used items are also sold. And then there's the food: thousands of pies, cookies, cakes, breads, and rolls are baked; home-preserved jams, jellies, pickles, and relishes line the food booths.

The proceeds are donated directly to the Mennonite Central Committee, which uses the funds to provide food and other necessities to war-torn or famine-stricken areas around the globe. Many thousands of visitors attend the Relief Sales each year—a good time for a good cause.

INDEX

Bread, Rolls, and Doughnuts

Amish Breakfast Puffs 37
Bagels 37
Banana Nut Bread 38
Basic White Bread 39
Chocolate Baking Powder
    Doughnuts 40
Chocolate Zucchini Bread 41
Church Cinnamon Rolls 42
Communion Bread
    (Unleavened) 42
Corn Bread 43
Dinner Rolls 44
Easy Cinnamon Rolls 45
Egg Bread 46
German Dark Rye Bread 47
Ginger Pumpkin Bread 48
Graham Crackers 49
Herb Biscuits 49
Honey Oatmeal Bread 50
Long Johns 51
Oatmeal Bread 52
Oven-Baked Doughnuts 53
Peasant Bread 54
Pluck-Its 55
Pumpkin Bread 56
Pumpkin Cinnamon Rolls with
    Caramel Frosting 56
Quick and Easy Pizza Crust 58
Refrigerator Dinner Rolls 58
Soda Crackers 59
Soft Pretzels 60
Sourdough Bread 60
Sourdough English Muffins 62
Sourdough Pancakes 63
Sourdough Rye Bread 63
Sourdough Starter 61
Sticky Buns 64
Sweet Cream Buns 66
Sweet Johnny Cake 67
Walnut Bread with Streusel
    Filling 67
Wheat Bread 68
Wheat Bread (Large Batch) 69
Wheat Muffins 69
Whole Wheat Crackers 70
Whole Wheat Quick Buttermilk
    Bread 70
Zucchini Bread 71
Zwieback 71

Breakfast Treats

Amish Breakfast Casserole 9
Amish Breakfast Pizza 9
Amish Coffee Cake 10
Apple Cinnamon Granola 10
Apple Fritters 11
Apple Oatmeal 11
Bacon, Egg, and Cheese
    Casserole 12
Basic Granola 12
Berry Muffins 13
Blackberry Syrup 13
Blueberry Oatmeal Muffins 14
Breakfast Crunch Bars 14
Bubbat 15
Buckwheat Pancakes 15
Buttermilk Biscuits with Sausage
    Gravy 16
Buttermilk Pancakes 17
Cheesy Breakfast Casserole 17
Corn Fritters 18
Cornmeal Mush 18
Cottage Cheese Fritters 19
Cottage Cheese Pancakes 19
Cracked Wheat Cereal 19
Creamed Eggs on Toast 20
Drop Biscuits 20
Dutch Babies 21
Easy Buttermilk Pancakes 21
Fastnachts 22
Four-Week Refrigerator Bran
    Muffins 23
Grandma's Granola 24
Grape Syrup 24
Homemade Graham "Nuts"
    Cereal 25
Homemade Maple Syrup 25
Hush Puppies 26
Oatmeal Muffins 26
Oatmeal Pancakes 27
Peanut Butter Granola 28
Poached Eggs 28
Potato Crust Pie 29
Potato Pancakes I 30
Potato Pancakes II 30
Potato Pancakes III 31

Quick Cinnamon Breakfast
    Fans 31
Sausage and Egg Casserole 32
Scrapple 32
Stovetop Breakfast Casserole 33
Tomato Gravy 33
Tomato Sour Cream Gravy 34
Traditional Biscuits 34

Desserts

Amish Cottage Cheese Custard
    Pie 191
Amish Date and Oatmeal
    Cake 191
Amish No-Bake Cookies 192
Amish Friendship Bread
    Starter 192
Amish Friendship Bread 194
Amish Sugar Cookies 195
Amish Vanilla Pie 195
Amish Wedding Nothings 196
Angel Food Cake 197
Apple Coffee Cake 197
Apple Crisp 198
Apple Goodie 198
Applesauce Half-Moon Pies 199
Applesauce Spice Cake 199
Baked Apples 200
Berry Dumplings 200
Black and Blue(berry)
    Cobbler 201
Bread Pudding 202
Butter Crust Pastry 202
Buttermilk Pie 203
Busy Day Cobbler 203
Cake Pie 204
Carmel-Apple Dumplings 205
Carmel Popcorn 206
Carmel Pudding 206
Carrot Cake with Cream Cheese
    Frosting 207
Cherry Pie 208
Chocolate Chip Cookies for a
    Crowd 208
Chocolate Chip Pie 209

Chocolate Cornstarch
    Pudding 209
Chocolate Frosting 210
Chocolate Fudge 210
Chocolate Sauerkraut Cake 211
Christmas Cake 212
Christmas Sugar Cookies 213
Coffee Cake 214
Crackletop Molasses Cookies 215
Cream Cheese Bars 215
Cream Puffs 216
Easy Coconut Macaroons 217
Fresh Peach Pie 217
Funeral Pie 218
Ginger Cake 219
Ginger Cookies 219
Graham Cracker Fluff 220
Hunt Pies 221
Lemon Buttercream Frosting 221
Lemon Meringue Pie 222
Lemon Sponge Pudding 223
Mama's Pie Crust 224
Minted Nuts 224
Mix-in-the-Pan Chocolate
    Cake 225
Never-Fail Pie Crust 225
Nut Balls 226
Old-Fashioned Custard Pie 226
Orange Frosted Cookies 227
Peach Custard Pie 228
Peanut Brittle 228
Pear Pudding Cake 229
Pecan Pie 230
Popcorn Balls 230
Popcorn Birthday Cake 231
Pumpkin Coconut Pudding
    Dessert 232
Quick Leftover Rice Pudding 232
Revel Bars 233
Rhubarb Chess Pie 234
Rhubarb Coffee Cake 234
Rhubarb Custard Pie 235
Rice Pudding 235
Rocky Road Fudge 236
Seven-Layer Cookies 236

Shoo-Fly Pie 237
Snickerdoodles 237
Strawberry Pie 238
Strawberry Tapioca Pudding 239
Super Easy Chocolate Cake 239
Sweet Zucchini Bread 240
Tapioca Fluff 240
Vanilla Cornstarch Pudding 241
Whoopie Pies 241

Main Dishes and Casseroles

A Husband's Delight 139
Amish Dressing I 139
Amish Dressing II 140
Amish Dressing III 141
Amish Dressing IV 142
Baked Chicken and Apples 143
Baked Macaroni and Cheese 144
Beef and Noodle Bake 144
Beef and Noodle Casserole 145
Beef and Vegetable Loaf 145
Braised Beef Cubes 146
Busy Day Ham Casserole 146
Cabbage Casserole with
    Hamburger 147
Calico Beans 148
Chicken and Pimento Loaf 148
Chicken Party Buns 149
Chicken Potpie 149
Chicken Tetrazzini 151
Creamy Chicken Bake 152
Creamy Noodle and Hamburger
    Casserole 153
Enchilada Casserole 154
Fidget Pie 154
Filsa 155
German Meatballs and
    Sauerkraut 156
German Rye Meatballs 157
Ham Loaf 158
Hamburger Gravy and Mashed
    Potatoes 159
Hamburger Macaroni 159
Hamburger Pie with Onion
    Biscuits 160

Hamburger Roll-Ups with Gravy 161
Haystack Supper 162
Hobo Dinner 163
Hot Sauce Beef and Rice 163
Individual Beef Potpies 164
Konigsberger Klopse 165
Lasagna Casserole 166
Leftover Turkey Croquettes 166
Liver and Vegetable Skillet 167
Meatballs and Gravy 167
Meatballs and Mushroom Gravy 168
Meat Loaf and Mashed Potatoes 168
Meat Loaf and Potatoes 169
Muffin Burgers 169
Old-Fashioned Beef Hash 170
Oven-Baked Chicken I 170
Oven-Baked Chicken II 171
Oven-Baked Chicken III 171
Overnight Ham and Macaroni Casserole 172
Oyster Filling 173
Penny Supper 173
Pizza Casserole 174
Poor Man's Steak 174
Porcupine Meatballs 175
Pot Roast 176
Quick and Easy Ranch Baked Beans 177
Ribbon Meat Loaf 177
Rice Krispie Chicken 178
Rice Krispie Hamburger Bake 178
Scalloped Oysters 179
Shepherd's Pie 179
Snitz and Knepp 180
Sour Cream Beef and Noodle Bake 181
Super-Duper Noodle Casserole 181
Swiss Steak 182
Tamale Pie Casserole 183
Tuna Casserole 184

Tuna, Cheese, and Rice Muffins 184
Tuna Macaroni Casserole 185
Tuna Stroganoff 185
Tuna Swiss Pie 186
Turkey Supreme 186
Wigglers 187
Yum-a-Setta 187

Mixes and Miscellaneous

Amish Church Peanut Butter Spread 245
Amish Church Peanut Butter Spread (Small Batch) 245
Barbecue Sauce 245
Barbecue Sauce for Chicken 246
Better Butter 246
Bird Suet That Won't Go Rancid 246
Brined-in-the-Jar Dill Pickles 247
Catsup 247
Chicken-Flavored Rice Mix 248
Chow Chow 248
Frozen Strawberry Jam 249
Fruit Drops 249
Homemade Baking Powder 250
Homemade Grape Juice 250
Hot Chocolate Mix I 250
Hot Chocolate Mix II 251
Lemonade Concentrate 251
Master Biscuit Mix 252
  Drop Biscuits 252
  Cheese Biscuits 252
  Rolled Biscuits 252
  Pancakes or Waffles 253
  Quick Pizza Crust 253
  Super Easy Doughnuts 253
Master Brownie Mix 254
  Brownies 254
  Chewy Chocolate Cookies 255
Master Cornbread Mix 255
  Corn Muffins 256
  Cornbread 256
  Honey Butter 256
Master Oatmeal Muffin Mix 256

  Oatmeal Muffins 257
Master Pancake Mix 257
  Basic Pancakes 257
  Oven Puff Pancakes 258
Mexican Rice Mix 258
Orange Float Mix 259
Onion Dip Mix 259
Onion-Flavored Rice Mix 260
Playdough 260
Ranch-Style Dressing and Dip Mix 261
Red Beet Eggs 262
Snitz 262
Spicy and Sweet Barbecue Sauce 263
Vegetable Dip Mix 263
White Sauce Mix 264
  Basic White Sauce 264

Salads and Dressings

Basic Oil and Vinegar Salad Dressing 95
Beet and Apple Salad 95
Carrot and Pineapple Salad 95
Chicken Salad 96
Coleslaw 96
Cottage Cheese Salad 97
Cream Dressing 97
Creamy Pea Salad 97
Creamy Ribbon Salad 98
Dutch Slaw 99
French Dressing 99
Fruit Salad Poppy Seed Dressing 100
Fruit Salad with Dressing 100
German Potato Salad 101
Honey Dressing 101
Hot Chicken Salad 102
Layered Salad 102
Macaroni Salad 103
Our Molded Jell-O Salad 103
Plain and Tasty Potato Salad 104
Rhubarb Salad 105
7-Up Salad 105
Sauerkraut Salad 106

Sour Cream Cucumber Slices 106
Sour Cream Dressing 107
Strawberry Pretzel Salad 107
Summer Salad 108
Sweet Potato Salad 108
Tangy Marinated Bean Salad 109
Thousand Island Dressing 109
Triple-Layer Salad 109
Wilted Dandelion Salad 110
Zesty Oil and Vinegar
    Dressing 111

Soups and Stews

Amish Bacon Bean Soup 75
Amish Church Soup 75
Amish Egg Soup 75
Baked Beef Stew 76
Beef and Barley Soup 76
Broccoli and Cottage
    Cheese Soup 77
Cabbage Chowder 77
Chicken Chowder 78
Chunky Beef Vegetable Soup
    to Feed a Hundred 79
Coffee Beef Stew 80
Corn Chowder 81
Cream of Cabbage Soup 81
Easy Hamburger Stew 82
Farmer's Favorite Soup 82

Five-Hour Beef Stew 83
Fruit Soup 83
Hasenpfeffer Stew 84
Knepp Soup 84
Lentil Soup 85
Meatball Chowder 86
Meatball Stew 87
Mennonite Stew 88
Potato Rivvel Soup 88
Shipwreck Stew 89
Stonaflesch 90
Tramp Soup 90
Vegetable Stew 91
White Bean Soup 91

Vegetables and Side Dishes

Baked Acorn Squash 115
Baked Acorn Squash with
    Hamburger Filling 115
Baked Onions 116
Baked Sweet Potatoes 116
Baked Turnips 117
Barley Casserole 117
Broccoli Cheese Casserole 118
Broccoli with Cheese Sauce 118
Celery and Almonds 119
Celery and Cheese Casserole 119
Cheese and Bread Casserole 120
Company Scalloped Potatoes 120

Cooked Beets 121
Corn Pie 121
Cottage Cheese-Filled Noodles 122
Creamed Celery and
    Almonds 122
Creamed Tomatoes and
    Onions 123
Garden Supper Casserole 124
Green Beans and Hot Dogs 124
Green Beans and New
    Potatoes 125
Green Beans with Mustard
    Sauce 125
Homemade Egg Noodles 126
Knepp and Asparagus 126
Onion Fritters 127
Potluck Potato Casserole 127
Roesti (Browned Potatoes) 128
Sautéed Onions and Apples 129
Scalloped Carrots 129
Scalloped Corn 130
Scalloped Rice with Cheese
    Sauce 131
Spinach Pie 132
Stewed Tomatoes and
    Dumplings 133
Summer Squash Casserole 134
Zucchini and Corn Side Dish 134
Zucchini Casserole 135